By the author of

Know The City and  ess

CHRISTOPHER STOAKES

GET TO THE POINT

HOW TO WRITE WELL AT WORK

ΧΦΣ

British library cataloguing-in-publication data

A catalogue record for this book is available from the British Library.

Published by:
Christopher Stoakes Ltd
Marlowe House
Hale Road
Wendover
Bucks
HP22 6NE

ISBN: 978-0-9574946-3-3

First published November 2013.

Printed and bound in Great Britain.

Written by Christopher Stoakes. Edited and researched by Viola Joseph.

Written, edited and researched at Scripto KT, Mews WO and Astoria DM.

© Christopher Stoakes 2013

The CSL logo incorporating the Greek device is a registered trade mark.

What this book is about

Writing is one of the key factors in professional success. It is one of the ways in which managers and clients appraise you. It will have a direct impact on your career. Write well and clients and colleagues will rate you. Write badly and it could harm your prospects. This book will help you develop a straightforward and compelling style that will enable you to get your points across simply and quickly.

Who this book is for

Bosses say the young people they recruit cannot write. But young people are used to communicating and expressing themselves more than ever before. And the professions they go into, like law, accountancy and management consultancy, attract the very best graduates. These young people can certainly write.

So what's going on? This book addresses that issue. It explains how to write well at work. Whether or not you have been taught to write well at school, this book will help you develop the right techniques for work. By applying some basic principles, tips and techniques, it will help you write in a way that bosses and clients want.

Who this book is by

Chris Stoakes is a master of language. He also knows the world of business. His books on business subjects such as the financial markets, commercial awareness and the law are hugely popular, especially amongst young people, for their clarity of expression and simplicity of style.

Chris has been writing professionally for thirty years. He has been by-lined in the quality national papers, his words have been quoted in Parliament and he has edited a wide variety of business, finance and legal publications. He is also an award-winning poet.

Chris knows the professional world. He has been a lawyer, a partner in a City law firm and a management consultant. He trains professionals in how to write. He is a qualified teacher and an MBA tutor.

It's this experience and viewpoint that Chris brings to bear in *Get To The Point*.

Chris was educated at Charterhouse and Oxford where he read law.

CONTENTS

WHY READ THIS BOOK   vii

CHAPTER 1: NO MARKS   1

CHAPTER 2: DO WHAT THE READER WANTS   7

CHAPTER 3: THE FIRST DRAFT OF ANYTHING IS RUBBISH   17

CHAPTER 4: GET TO THE POINT   29

CHAPTER 5: DISMANTLE THE SCAFFOLDING   39

CHAPTER 6: SPACE MATTERS   45

CHAPTER 7: EMAIL IS KRYPTONITE   51

CHAPTER 8: THINGS PEOPLE GET WRONG   59

CHAPTER 9: KEEPING IT SIMPLE   69

CHAPTER 10: ~~CONCLUSION~~   81

INDEX   85

Why Read This Book

This book could change your life. It's ridiculous but it's true. And that's because one of the biggest things preventing young people from getting the job they want or being successful in a role is the way they write.

At work the way you write is at the heart of the way you communicate. In the workplace you will do more communicating by writing than anything else: emails, memos, reports, even letters. It far outweighs the number of times you will speak memorably in a meeting or on the phone. It will endure for longer too. In fact later on in this book I tell you to assume your emails will last for ever and be read by everyone.

Even if you do presentations, how you write them (which includes how you structure them) will determine their success even more than the way in which you deliver them. Great delivery with poor content is still a poor presentation. Great content poorly delivered will still provide some value (although of course you want to do both well: both the writing and the delivery; this book is about the writing).

How you write is visible to everyone, your boss and clients alike. So this book is aimed at young professionals just starting out on their careers, who know they need to write well but aren't sure how to do it.

And why should you listen to me? I'm a professional (a lawyer, who has also been a management consultant and held various senior roles in law firms heading up marketing, training and knowledge management). I'm a professional writer who writes books like this that people praise for their clarity. I'm also a teacher and trainer. I have a PGCE, taught for ten years on an MBA and train professional people in how to write. Crucially and unusually for someone in a professional role, I've been a journalist and editor. That's where I learnt what I know about writing. It wasn't from being a lawyer.

The Big Disconnect

Here's the thing. Your generation is incredibly articulate. You text each other all the time. You have facebook pages. You tweet. You're used to being asked for your opinion and used to giving it. Your generation consumes and communicates. You know how you want things and you're not afraid to say so. You are great at getting your point across.

Yet bosses say that the young people they hire these days don't know how to write. (They also say they can't read either, which is possibly part of the same issue.)

For me this is the Big Disconnect. Bosses say you can't write. But I believe you can. So what's going on?

I think the answer is this. You can write. But not in the way they want. And this is worse the better educated you are. I work with some of the brightest graduates from the best UK universities. They write well and they know they do. Yet they often get criticised in the workplace for the way they write. And the fact they have been well educated makes the issue worse. Because they know they can write. So why are they being criticised? If you know you can write you are less willing to respond to someone who says you can't.

So this book teaches you how to write for the workplace. It helps you write the way that bosses want.

And this, I think, could unlock your career.

Get to the point

All right, Chris. So get to the point. So I don't have to read through this book (and certainly not to the end), what does it say?

Let's start with two things.

First, poor writing is a reflection of poor thinking. Professionals grapple with difficult disciplines and challenging issues. Our areas of expertise are complex. Then, on top of that, we have to apply them to a particular set of issues. The answer may be difficult to pin down. So we use writing to work out what it is. But then we fail to go back and rewrite what we have written with the answer up front. Or we don't have time to. So we send out our first draft, which shows all of our thinking and meanders to a solution, and the reader finds it hard to follow (and isn't interested in all of our thinking anyway). This is why we come across as pompous. We fail to translate the language of our specialism into everyday language that others can understand.

Second, being good at writing is a mindset. The mindset is to be open to change. If you think you know how to write you have no room left to learn. If you think that writing is a lifelong learning experience you will always improve.

I've been writing professionally for 30 years. Yet every time I look back at something I've written (which is mercifully rarely) it looks hideously clumsy to me. After reading two sentences I put it aside. That doesn't mean to say that when I wrote it it wasn't the very best I could make it. But I've moved on since then. What was good then isn't any more. I'm still learning. I rewrite my books all the time.

I'll be rewriting this one in due course. If you can be bothered, tell me what's wrong with it, preferably in a way that will help me improve it so I can make it better next time for the next round of readers.

CHAPTER 1

NO MARKS

Who is your reader? – why are they reading (what you are about to write)? – the three reasons why people read – entertainment – information – action – the reader comes first – the customer is king – the professional adviser's job is to make the client's life easier – your first reader is your boss – writing as a student to be assessed – the purpose of writing at work is different – there are no marks in business – state of transition – how we are taught to write at school – essays – introduction – argument (thesis) – counter-argument (antithesis) – conclusion – purpose – assessment – showing your working – writing for yourself – the reader knows the answer – why essays don't work in business – at work the reader doesn't know the answer – the reluctant reader

Before you even begin to put pen to paper you need to ask yourself two fundamental questions:

- Who is your reader?
- Why are they reading (what you are about to write)?

Why people read

People read for three reasons.

For entertainment This is about reading for relaxation. It's what I call the book on the beach. It's reading for entertainment and it's principally about reading fiction. That's not what we're concerned with here although experienced practitioners of the novelist's art (such as Ernest Hemingway and Stephen King) can teach us things that will help when writing at work – as we'll see. After all, if you can entertain as a by-product of the real purpose of why you are writing, that will make your readers even happier to persevere.

However, at work, people read for the other two reasons.

For information This is when people need to be aware of something but are not expected to take any actual action as a result. The piece is not directed at them but they need to be kept in the loop. For example, you may copy in your boss so that she knows you have done something she wanted you to do. It's what the letters 'cc' mean. They come from when letters and memos were typed on actual mechanical typewriters and the force of the keys made a 'carbon copy' on a sort of tracing paper underneath.

For action This is when someone needs to do something and your piece helps them decide what to do. This is what we are principally concerned with in this book. It's the principal purpose of writing at work.

The reader comes first

Now let's go back to the first question: who is your reader?

I am assuming that you are reading this because you are pursuing a professional career. This means that you will have clients. Maybe not immediately, but certainly in due course. Then your clients will be your readers.

It is a cardinal rule of business that the client (or customer) always comes first. The various clichés include: 'The customer is king' and 'Customers are always right, even when they are wrong' and so on. They may be clichés, but that doesn't make them any less true.

Your job as professional adviser is to make your client's life easier. In business parlance your job is to provide solutions. This means you are writing to help the client. In doing so your job is to make your writing as easy for the client to read as possible. So, to recast these various clichés: 'The reader is king'; 'The reader is always right'. We'll be coming back to this again and again.

Your first reader is your boss

When you are starting out on your career your first reader is your boss (your supervisor or your manager). The reason you are writing is because she needs to do something with your piece (action).

Just because it's for your boss doesn't make it any less important. In fact your boss can have more of a direct impact on your career. So your boss is your first client. And all of the skills you will need to develop when dealing directly with clients you can start to hone by trying them out on your boss first. And one of these is how you write.

The writing you do at work will be very different from writing at school, college or university. For a start, the purpose is completely different. As a student you were writing to be assessed. The purpose was so that the reader could assess your knowledge of the subject in hand in order to award a mark. In a sense you were writing for yourself. Your job was to get the best mark you could. Your assessor knew the subject better than you did. That's how he or she could mark your work. You weren't writing to tell the assessor anything he or she didn't already know.

Writing at work is different.

Here you are writing for clients (either internal clients like your boss and other colleagues; or real external clients). The point is this: there are no marks in business. Either the piece does the job or it doesn't. In this sense writing at work is all or nothing. Just as professional advisers have to get the answer right, so it's not enough to get it mainly right or largely right or 70% right. Yet as a student 70% probably got you a distinction. At work you need 100% or it's a nil. If you're writing isn't as easy for the reader to read as possible it's a zero.*

Now, to an extent when you are starting out, your boss is judging your state of knowledge. But rarely will a boss give you a piece of work to do just to test you. Mainly it's because your boss is a busy person who has asked you to do a task for a particular business purpose, for instance because a client has asked for it. Even if a client hasn't, how well you write for your boss will determine how quickly you will be unleashed on real client work. Since this is why you have been employed, the sooner it happens the better. This means that in all of your writing you are writing for real, even if a particular piece of work isn't going directly to a client. Your boss or other colleagues are going to be relying on what you say. Your task is to make their lives easier.

Why does the reader need to read what you have written?

All organisations have clients or customers, whether they are big businesses, corner shops, parts of central or local government or charities. In life we all serve each other. Businesses spend a lot of money finding out what clients want and then providing them with goods or services to meet those needs. The best professional advisers put this at the heart of what they do: finding out the specific client's need. In fact a good definition of marketing is meeting clients' needs profitably: identifying those needs then satisfying them at a cost that doesn't incur a loss for the provider.

So with writing.

You need to work out why the client / reader needs your piece. What is the question or issue he needs addressed? Why does he think it needs addressing? What is he going to do as a result of what you write?

Once you know the answers to these questions you can begin to deploy your body of professional expertise to solve the client's issues. I come back to this later.

For now I just want you to see that you are in a state of transition, from student to professional. I expect you were a successful student. This means you know how to write. The problem is that the writing you know how to do and have mastered is not what is required from now on.

Essays

I don't know about you but I was taught at school to write essays.

You set out what you are going to do in an Introduction (In this essay I am going to examine the issue of whether…) and the key points you are going to cover. Then you set each point out.

If you are writing an essay in the classical French sense ('essay' comes from the French to 'try' as in to make an intellectual attempt or argument) each key point comprises a thesis (argument) and an antithesis (counter-argument). And once you have exhausted all of your arguments and counter-arguments you sweep the whole thing together in a grand baroque conclusion where you come down on one side of the proposition or the other.

In actual fact what you conclude doesn't matter. The students who come down on one side won't get 100% and those who favour the other get 0%. It doesn't work like that. What you will be assessed on is the quality of the information you have at your disposal and how you have marshalled and deployed it in support of your arguments. It's a bit like 'showing your working' in maths. As long as the assessor can see that your approach is correct it doesn't matter nearly as much if you happen to make a mistake in the calculation itself and the actual answer isn't quite right. You will still get the bulk of the marks for having demonstrated the right methodology.

Why essays don't work in business

This doesn't work in business for one very good reason. The reader is not reading what you have written because they know the answer and want to test whether you do too (or at least have the right methodology to arrive at it).

The reader is reading because he or she doesn't know the answer and wants to find out what it is – preferably as quickly as possible. Even your boss, who knows more than you do, may be asking for a piece of writing to meet a specific client need which she hasn't thought about in great depth, so she is asking you to do so. You have the time. She doesn't. She is busy on other things. So she will be relying on your deeper analysis. She will be relying on what you write.

Let's say your boss has asked you to draft a memorandum that will form the basis of a piece of advice for a client. The closer you can make that memo to the finished article the better for you, your boss and the client.

What you as the writer need to do is to convey throughout the memo the relevance of what you are saying while providing the client with the information he needs in order to know what to do next once he's stopped reading. For instance, to be useful (and keep the reader's attention) you need to set out the options (for what to do next) and enough information for the reader to be able to choose with confidence between them. That's because someone reading for action needs to know:

- What he needs to do
- Why he needs to do it
- What the risks and obstacles are
- What the next steps are

These points are not a template for every piece of writing you do. That will depend on the specific issues and the specific client. All I am doing here is showing you how different this approach is from writing an essay.

I've said already that you need to be quick in the way you set out and tackle these items. This is because, unlike the assessor whose job it is to read your writing, your readers at work have many other things they need to do, almost all of which are more important in their eyes than reading what you have written.

In other words you are writing for reluctant readers – people who would rather not be reading your piece at all, as we shall see.

CHAPTER 2

DO WHAT THE READER WANTS

The reader wants to stop reading as soon as possible – no one in business has time – what you have written will always be subservient – the continuous internal loop – why am I reading this? – can I stop now? – if not, then when? – what am I supposed to do about it next? – what else do I need to know in order to be able to do that? – no introduction – no conclusion – make your conclusion your opening paragraph – no footnotes – editing an article by a Brazilian lawyer – put footnotes in the text – no bibliographies – doing what the reader wants – err on the side of caution – what is the reader going to do next – putting the reader first – not taking criticism of your writing style personally – writing as continuous improvement – think reader – Philip Larkin – asking the reader – supporting the reader / client's strategy – three reasons why what we write doesn't please readers – you're new – the language of your discipline – using writing to work out the answer

The terrible truth is that for the most part your readers at work don't want to be reading what you have written at all.

Your reader wants to stop reading as soon as possible

Business readers want to stop reading what you have written as soon as possible so that they can (a) do something about it if necessary or (b) get on to the next job on their To Do List.

This is because no one – especially in business – has time. Everything is immediate. This isn't something new – although it's fair to say that the internet has accelerated response times exponentially. But even in the old days before telex and fax (themselves redundant technologies) business was fast, or at least as fast as it could be. In the City of London, for example, there were six letter deliveries a day. You could send a letter in the City by first post (about 7.30am) and expect a reply by 11am that same morning. Business has always been fast-paced within the technological constraints of the day.

Everyone at work is busy. They have things they need to do. Those things are often urgent. And reading what you have written is not one of them. People may need to read your piece in order to get done what they are tasked with doing. But reading your piece is not an end in itself. It is a means to something else. So what you have written will always be subservient. It will always be incidental. It is meant to do a job and to do that job as quickly as possible so it can be set aside as soon as possible.

The continuous internal loop

What is going on in your reader's head is a continuous internal loop that is posing your reader the same four questions round and round and round:

- Why am I reading this?
- Can I stop now? If not, then when?
- What am I supposed to do about it next?
- What else do I need to know in order to be able to do that?

This loop is going round inside the reader's head subconsciously, driven by the reader's lack of time and the need to get on with the next job. These four questions start to shape your writing and its contents to provide the reader with what he wants (rather than what you want to tell him).

You can see now why the essay (mentioned in the previous chapter) doesn't work. If your boss and the client are in such a hurry, they are not going to stand for a grand baroque conclusion that comes at the end. What they want to be told is the answer, as up front as possible, and what to do about it (if they were reading for entertainment this wouldn't be the case – even if they wanted to find out what happened at the story's end).

No conclusion and no introduction

You can see immediately that the essay structure is wrong for our purpose here.

You do not need a formal introduction. You may need an opening sentence or two reminding the reader of the context. The chances are you're responding to a client's request. So the client knows why you are writing. Nor do you want to hold back with your answer to the end. It follows that, if you are saying up front what the solution to the client's issue is, you won't need a conclusion either.

If you are prone to writing a conclusion, here's a good tip. Take that paragraph and make it your opening statement. You may need to adjust the wording a bit. But it will immediately give your piece of writing more purpose and punch. It will make it a faster read. And fast is good in business.

No footnotes and no bibliographies

Two other things while we're getting rid of the baggage of school and uni. No footnotes and no bibliographies.

When you are writing a doctoral thesis you need both. Footnotes make you look academic. But look at most footnotes and they are unnecessary. They take the eye away from where it was on the page, divert it to some small script at the bottom, then the reader has to go back up the page and find the right place again in the main text. That's dangerous. It's a distraction. It's an invitation to the reader to give up completely.

As a young editor I was in charge of a magazine on international financial law. It published articles by eminent lawyers from around the world. I received one from a top Brazilian banking lawyer. It was all about taking security (which is what banks often do when they make loans). The footnotes were longer than the article. So when the typesetter laid it out on the page (this was in the days before computers took over) the article stopped a third of the way down and the rest of each page was footnotes. It looked awful and was almost unreadable because every sentence was footnoted. So I rewrote it to incorporate as many of these footnotes in the text as possible. The unnecessary ones I left out.

When the article appeared in the magazine the Brazilian lawyer was not a happy man. But he was in Sao Paulo, I was in London and so we were unlikely ever to meet. So I didn't care. What I cared about were my readers – mainly bankers and in-house lawyers who worked in the legal departments of banks and companies. These were commercial people. They didn't want an academic treatise. There were plenty of academic journals about on the market and I wasn't about to turn my publication into one of them. But it wasn't the Brazilian lawyer's fault either. It's a country with a strong academic tradition in law and where the top lawyers in the best law firms are often professors at the local university too. Footnoting a piece is what you do when you want academics to take it seriously. However, my job was to put my readers first. They wanted practical stuff. Footnotes sent out the wrong message and made the piece unreadable.

Again, here's a suggestion. If you use footnotes, put them in brackets in the text. Soon you'll find you need far fewer then you thought. You may even cure yourself of the footnote disease completely.

Bibliographies are not quite so bad. But again their purpose is academic: to show you've done the desk research and to give attribution to others' ideas. They show how well read you are.

In the workplace you only need to refer to other things (such as a court case if you're a lawyer) so that the reader can check out what you're saying. So either refer to it in the text (at the point where it's most relevant) or not at all.

If you need to refer to something at such length that it would distort your piece, put it in an appendix at the back. Then you can make it as long as you like. That's because the reader is unlikely to read it.

Doing what the reader wants

I mentioned earlier that the reader is your client and the client is always right. All organisations have customers or clients. Whether an organisation delivers what the customer wants is a subjective judgement that is entirely in the customer's mind. If the customer complains it means the organisation has either failed to deliver the required goods or services or failed to communicate to the customer why what has been delivered is better suited to the customer's needs.

The lesson for us is that we must do what our reader wants. So far I have assumed your reader wants the answer as quickly and succinctly as possible. We shall see that what this means in practice is simple, direct language, and this is generally what commercial clients want (people who work in business).

But there may be exceptions. For example, a private banker or fund manager serving a very wealthy individual (a high-net-worth as the rich are called) may discover that the client doesn't want something short and to the point. The client may feel he is only getting his money's worth if the banker or fund manager provides him with a voluminous report discussing recent trends in the financial markets and their impact on the client's portfolio. There are clients like that. And if that is what they want then that is what you must do.

Most business people do not want that. They want things quick and short and immediate. But there is a wider lesson here and it is that you need to err on the side of caution until you know your reader really well.

Err on the side of caution

In the workplace assume that anyone older or more senior than you will be more traditional. So do what they would want. Follow the rules of grammar (we'll look at these later). Write sentences with verbs in them. Be formal until you know it's all right not to be.

Look at their communications. Study their use of language. What salutations do they use (Hi? Dear? None at all?). Do they use first names or surnames? Even if they use none at all that doesn't mean you can: more senior people tend to be too busy to top and tail their communications with names.

These are the things you need to study for clues as to what is considered appropriate at your particular place of work and at your level of seniority. Otherwise you risk offending your superiors or having them think less of you which damages your credibility and the impact of your message.

But where you do know the reader (a work colleague or your boss, for instance) you can be much more direct with the language you use. You can break the rules to a greater extent if they won't mind.

What is the reader going to do next?

I mentioned earlier that you need to think about why the client wants or needs to read your piece. What is it he needs to do next, having read it? What does he need to know in order to do that?

And you need to think about what may happen to your piece. Who else may need to see it? Who else will your reader need to pass it to? What is that person's state of knowledge and what do they too need to know?

At this point you need to remember that you probably know more about the topic than they do, and not everything you know is necessarily going to be relevant or needed by them. You are already being selective about what you need to include.

What this is about is putting the reader first.

Putting the reader first

This is actually more significant than you might think, for this reason.

I don't know why, but we take how we write extremely seriously, possibly because it is an expression of our true selves, of our personality. And I'm not just talking about professional writers. All of us do. If someone criticises your writing style it's almost like a personal attack. On the one hand we feel exposed. On the other there's not much we feel we can do about it: that's the way I write; I can't help it. Having your writing criticised is almost like being told you are ugly. It is wounding and deeply offensive.

However, this is something you need to overcome, by putting the reader's needs above yours.

Writing is continuous improvement

The first step to writing well is to grasp that you are the reader's servant. The spotlight is on him and what he wants and needs. How the reader gets it – what you write and how you write it – is only incidental.

Remember what it feels like when you do something stupid at work? You feel all eyes are on you. Everyone knows. In fact it usually isn't the case. People don't know. They are too wrapped up in themselves and the impression they are making. And if they do, they are probably thinking: that could so easily have been me.

So with writing. Nobody cares how you write as long as they get what they want from it. Only if they don't, only if it makes their lives laborious or takes too long or can't be easily understood, do they start to look at the writing itself and, therefore, who wrote it.

This is a good reason not to feel self-conscious about how you write, and also not to feel too precious about it either. It's what I call: Think Reader.

I know this is far more easily said than done because I, too, have had to learn it the hard way. My first reader is always my editor. I learnt the hard way that my editor is always right. I used to argue with her and now I don't. I try instead to get to the heart of her criticism so that I can address it and correct what I've done.

But it isn't just my editor who is right. Any reader – or, rather, anyone to whom my writing is addressed – is right. In this sense writing is never finished. We just run out of time. You arrive at an optimal mix of effort and output. After all, writing is just one of the things we have to do in the service of the day job. Philip Larkin, the poet, once said that you don't write what you want to, only what you can. He also said of one of his poems (Church Going) that if he had known it was going to be so popular he would have spent more time making it better. So it is with the task of writing.

Asking the reader

So far I have drawn a pretty clear parallel between marketing (providing what the customer wants) and writing (writing what the reader wants). Let me go further. If you don't know what the reader wants when it comes to the way you write, ask them. It is a principal rule of business to make it your job to know what your customer wants. And to do that you need to ask them. Engaging customers or clients in a dialogue about what they are seeking by way of product or service is the best marketing a business can do. The best business people spend their time talking to customers to ensure their business remains relevant to the market.

I was once called in by a top professional services firm to help their professionals with their writing. One of the examples I came across was a 10-page letter setting out a complex explanation of a highly technical set of constraints telling the client what was preventing him from doing something. The final line of the letter read: 'That's the relevant background. But we're still not sure why you have asked the question'. This to my mind is a basic failure of client service. The work didn't provide a solution because it didn't identify or address the issue the client faced. Besides, professional people are expensive. They should not rack up huge costs in doing a piece of work if they do not know what the value to the client will be.

This was not just a failure of writing. It was a failure of basic business sense. When I asked, I think the answer I got was along the lines of: we didn't feel we could ask further in case we appeared stupid to the client because he'd already explained it once. To which the obvious reply is: how much angrier will he now feel having incurred all of your cost in producing such a technical piece of advice which may be irrelevant to his business goal?

How does writing support the client's strategy?

To answer this we need to look at what the workplace is about. People at work get things done. This is what business is about (and by business I include government and charities – any organisation that has a purpose; including schools and universities). All organisations have a strategy (a goal, a purpose, a sense of direction) and the job of the organisation is to achieve that strategy or, at least, to move closer towards the intended outcome. So anything written needs to support this.

Both information and action are relevant to business. Business is like flying a plane. You steer the plane on a course (strategy) in response to information coming at you through the instruments. The quality of writing in the workplace has a direct bearing on how quickly you receive and take in that information. Good decision-making flows from good information effectively presented. How information is presented is what this book is about.

Yet clients regularly complain that their advisers do not write in a clear and succinct way (is it any wonder, given the example above?) and bosses regularly complain the new recruits don't either. Why not? After all, it's not that hard a message to grasp, that you should write simply and succinctly.

Well, if you are a new recruit, you have my every sympathy. Because I think there are three reasons that hold you back.

Language as disguise

First, you're new to your profession. You don't know anything yet. But you want to give the impression you do. So you write the way you assume professional people should write. You use long words, long sentences and complex constructions – especially when you're not quite sure what you're talking about. You clothe your writing in a professional patina. It's a way of not being found out. Funnily enough, this fear of being found out never completely leaves us. All professionals feel it to some extent throughout their careers.

Older professionals may be poor role models anyway, since professional pomposity used to be the standard way of writing to clients. It's why estate agents refer to 'properties', 'purchasers' and 'vendors' rather than houses, buyers and sellers. There is an argument why estate agents should use this sort of language, and that's to impress upon people the magnitude of what they are doing. Buying or selling a house is likely to be the biggest individual financial transaction any of us do, so it's as well to be reminded of that.

But the best estate agents don't use this sort of language. The last time I used one he didn't. He sold my place within two weeks at exactly the price he put it on the market at, and it wasn't especially attractive or sellable. He did a great job. He used simple language. He called me the seller and the people who bought the buyer and the place in question a house not a property.

Steven Stark, a Harvard professor, says lawyers use pompous language to guard their economic interests and charge more. And he's a lawyer.

The language of your discipline

There's a second – and much more compelling – reason why professionals are often pompous. They forget to switch out of the language of their discipline. Every professional has a discipline, whether it's medicine, architecture, management consultancy, law, engineering, accountancy, surveying, chemistry, banking or public relations. It doesn't matter what it is. It's a body of expertise with its own language (it's said of economics that it only began to develop as a discipline in its own right when it started to develop a vocabulary to match).

As experts our job is to apply this body of expertise in our clients' interests (in the case of a research chemist, for example, developing new products for a pharmaceutical manufacturer). Whatever we write is hobbled by the fact that it is in a different language from English as it is spoken between people in the street. So we have to translate what we write into language anyone can understand (George Orwell said you should never use jargon, for this reason). But we often forget.

Lawyers, for example, use two different languages. One is English as it is written and spoken. The other looks like English but it is nothing of the sort.

Lawyers have to be precise in their use of language. In drawing up agreements that may have to endure for decades and be referred back to, they need to nail any ambiguity and cover any eventuality. To do that in precise terms requires the sort of language that has only a passing resemblance to everyday English. Acts of Parliament and decisions of courts are likewise written in a technical language that is almost unreadable to anyone but lawyers. And the mistake that lawyers make is to fail to switch out of this technical form of English (much of it dotted with Latin terms) when writing to clients.

In fact the best commercial lawyers write very simply: their clients, being busy business people, wouldn't tolerate it otherwise (but don't forget the rich client who wants the voluminous report).

Operating in the unknown

But there is a third reason why professional advisers write turgidly. We are often operating in the unknown. By definition as professionals we are dealing with complex, technical areas and applying our body of expertise to a client's particular circumstances.

When clients seek our advice it's usually because what is involved is complicated. It takes some thought. So we face two levels of complexity: that of our own discipline; and then its application to a particular set of facts. We have to grapple with tricky issues. Often the outcome is unclear and we need to think it through. Working out what we are trying to say is difficult. If it wasn't anyone could do it. Sometimes we fall back into technical jargon as a shorthand. Sometimes we write in stream-of-consciousness, charting our own thought processes, as we edge towards a solution.

The point is that we use writing to work out the answer. It's how most professionals work (by and large – maybe mathematicians don't, since they use figures). But for the rest of us we write our thoughts down as a way of working out what they are – which is fine. But, critically, we then fail to go back and rewrite what we have written so the reader can understand it.

In other words we don't go back and edit what we have written. Instead we send it out to the client as it is, when all we have done is use what we have written to work out, however messily, the answer.

And that isn't good enough, as we shall see.

CHAPTER 3

THE FIRST DRAFT OF ANYTHING IS RUBBISH

Hemingway – Stephen King – the first draft is for working out what the piece is about – daring to write badly – James Joyce – never send out your first draft – lack of time – fear of negligence – always leave your piece overnight – circadian rhythms – get someone else to read it – encourage specific comment – be prepared to act on criticism – learn not to care – why professionals don't seek feedback – cut the purple passages – re-imagining what you have written – be an editor yourself – be prepared to take time – Stephen Covey – the time spent will make you a better and quicker writer – Mark Twain

I didn't say it. Hemingway did. What he actually said was:

The first draft of anything is s***.

Please excuse the coarse language but that is actually what he wrote and – here's the funny thing – I bet you it wasn't his first draft either. I bet you that initially he really did write something like 'The first draft of anything is rubbish' but toned it up, made it more dramatic, by the use of coarse language. He wanted to give it emphasis. Now Hemingway was nothing if not a professional writer. And he was talking about himself as much as anyone else. And his prose is regarded as dead simple. He used simple words and simple constructions (in the main) which is why his prose is so fresh and modern.

OK, so we're not talking about writing great literature. But what Hemingway said applies equally to anything. You could say that fiction, being made up, is not as important as what we're talking about – writing in business. Because big sums of money and significant corporate strategies can turn on the effectiveness of how a point is put across in business.

To me there's no difference. It's all still about words. I believe a great writer is a great writer. Or, to put it another way, if you can inject some of these techniques from literature into your writing and make it more compelling without too much extra effort, isn't it worth doing if it means people are more likely to read and prize what you write? If you can write at work for work reasons but people enjoy how you write and enjoy reading what you have written, they are more likely to read it at all.

That's good because that's the aim. It could increase your influence in decisions, improve the organisation's decision-making ability and enhance your reputation and your career. That's a lot of benefit for just taking a bit of trouble with words. And, what's more, anyone can do it. That's a big advantage for almost nothing in today's competitive workplace environment. And even if being able to write well at work doesn't make such a big difference, writing badly certainly will.

Stephen King, the noted horror and sci-fi writer, says the first draft is when you work out what the story is actually about (he likens it to archaeology – unearthing the story and trying to get it entire out of the ground). Then – knowing what it is and how it ends – you rewrite it to put it in the right order so a reader can read it. He calls it two drafts and a polish. The polish is to work on individual words and phrases, to make the whole sparkle.

I don't like horror or sci-fi. But I still think King is a great writer and his book *On Writing* is well worth reading (in it, rather charmingly, he says he doesn't see why anyone should listen to what he has to say on the subject just because he is the biggest selling author on the planet. As he says, just because Colonel

Sanders sells a lot of fried chicken, you wouldn't necessarily ask him for the recipe).

So what has that got to do with us?

Everything. It is both liberating and a severe command.

Dare to write badly

It's liberating because you can write whatever you want and at least initially it doesn't matter. One of my favourite writers is Tracy Kidder. He writes non-fiction. His book about a team building a computer (*The Soul Of A New Machine*) won the Pulitzer prize and has become a case study in management books.

His editor Richard Todd in their book *Good Prose* said of Kidder that he is never afraid to write badly. What Todd means is that Kidder tries to get something, anything, down on paper which he and Todd can then go back and work on. At the same time, Todd says, Kidder kids himself (sorry) that this first draft is for real. It's a bit like golf. Golf is a stupid game. But unless you take it seriously it's not worth playing at all. So you know the first draft isn't for keeps. But it's of sufficient weight to be worth working on.

I see many people trying to produce a perfect first draft. They agonise over each sentence before moving on to the next. Experienced writers don't do this. They know the entire paragraph may be canned or changed so it's not worth sweating over words and sentences just yet. But what you need to get down are the big themes, the big ideas which are what will make your piece worth reading at all. That's what you're trying to capture and, preferably, in the right order (as we shall see editing is as much, if not more so, about the order as it is the actual words used themselves).

You may recall that old joke about James Joyce. A friend pops in to see him at the end of a day and Joyce is convulsed in creative agony.

'Why, what's up James?' his friend asks.

'It's the writing.'

'How much have you written today?'

'Seven words.'

'But, James, that's good for you.'

'Yes, but I don't know the order they go in.'

I mentioned at the end of the last chapter that professional disciplines are complex and that a lot of our job is actually working out the answer to a client's problem.

What we need to do then is to go back, knowing the outcome, and rewrite what we have written – just as Stephen King does – to make it as clear to the client as possible. This is how the meandering first draft that doesn't really know where it's going turns into that clearly expressed and superbly organised exposition that is the second draft. The first makes sense of the issue and identifies the solution. The second puts the solution centre-stage.

This brings us to the severe command.

Never, ever send out your first draft

That's why you should never send out the first draft of whatever you write. The first draft helps you work out what it is you want to say. The second draft helps you restate it in a way that will help the reader read it. You need to know what you are trying to say before you can put it in a form that someone will want to read.

But we seldom do this. Why not?

Two reasons.

The first is time, or lack of it. As professionals we are hard-pressed. Time costs money. Clients want to pay as little as possible. Going back and editing what we have done takes time and that increases cost. Far better to whack it out to the client than spend even more time and money making it intelligible.

The second is fear of negligence. It's called showing your working. It's what we were taught to do at school (you remember, for assessments). Professionals are scared of being sued for getting something wrong. Therefore by leaving everything in they make themselves safer. I don't believe this but we'll come to it later.

All I'm saying for now is that these are two reasons why we don't go back and rewrite. It's a huge mistake. The quickest and simplest way to improve your writing is to go back and rewrite it.

Always try to leave your first draft overnight

With anything long or that is of any substance at least try to sleep on it. The subconscious part of your brain will work on it while you're asleep and if you come at it afresh you will see it and read it differently.

For this reason it's worth being aware of your circadian rhythms (when you work best). For some people like me it's early in the morning. For others it's late at night when the day is behind them. Use that time to revise your piece.

Get someone else to read it

Better still, get someone else to read it. This won't always work (for instance if it's confidential – but you could get an intended recipient to give you a heads up). But on the whole getting a fresh pair of eyes will provide a completely different perspective (and you can offer to do the same for them).

Be careful. Only get someone else to read it if you don't want to waste their time or yours.

A waste of time is if someone reads it and says it's fine. Even worse if they read it and say it's really great.

Neither of these helps you make it better. Usually your piece isn't great. Your colleague just doesn't want to hurt your feelings. As I said, having people criticise your writing is like being told you're ugly. It really hurts! That's why they don't do it and why we don't ask people properly.

You have to encourage them.

'If I could improve it in one way what would that be?'

'If you'd written it what would you change?'

Always ask for specifics. Always ask for improvements.

Then you have to be brave. *You must be prepared to act on their criticism.* Whatever they say you mustn't take it personally. Above all you mustn't defend what you've written. If they don't like something they are right. Always.

If you really want to turn out polished prose you probably need an editor. I have been writing professionally for over thirty years and have had pieces published in all the major quality newspapers. Yet my stuff still gets hacked apart and reset. Not as much as it used to. But a large reason why the books I write sell a lot is because people find them easy to read. And that's because they are well-edited.

When I first started out as an editor I used to spend a lot of time down at the typesetters. This was long before computers and the transfer of words in soft copy. There the compositor would type the copy (the words to be printed) from the manuscripts (original articles) into a huge machine. This would spew out bromides (black words on bright shiny paper). The page-makeup artist would take these long strips of shiny paper and cut them (with a blade) and paste them (with glue) to fit in columns on cardboard templates. These templates were the pages from which the magazine or book would be printed.

My job was to go through these, check them and make cuts to the copy so that articles fitted perfectly on the page, removing orphans and widows (one word lines that made columns look ugly because they fell at the top or bottom). I needed to make cuts carefully to minimise the bromide re-runs and the page-makeup artist's job of lifting and repasting the galleys (as the strips laid to page were called), without distorting the author's intent – and remember, these were technical legal articles: so it was like doing a very complicated jigsaw puzzle. It's how my magazine was always forty-eight pages every month, regardless of how many articles we ran or how long they were. And why articles always started at the tops of the pages and finished always at the bottom, one, two, three or four pages later.

Sorting out the order of the articles in the magazine was called doing the flat plan and where parts of a magazine printed in colour – always an expensive option – and the rest printed mono (black), you were constantly juggling the order of the flat plan to make the best use of colour (printing colour pages in fours, but not sequentially) while getting the best order for the importance of the stories. It was the hardest bit of what I did but the most satisfying, like completing a jumbo crossword.

My first editors

At these particular typesetters the compositor was a large Irish lady called Mary. She worked with a dictionary permanently by her side. My magazine was a law magazine about international finance with articles by top lawyers.

Mary wasn't a lawyer. But she would regularly call me over and point out mistakes of grammar, syntax, style and spelling that these lawyers had made. She was stunningly brilliant at language. We fought regularly but in the end I always went with her suggestions. She was always right. She wasn't only typing the stuff in, she was reading it, understanding it, digesting it and critiquing it. This was a long time ago when I was young so, sadly, Mary must have died by now. I hope she knows I learnt a lot from her. Of course, my own copy got the full treatment and was picked apart remorselessly! Mary was my first editor.

Apart from Mary, I was also taught to write by an elderly ex-*Times* sub-editor (that's when I wasn't at the typesetters having my stuff taken apart by Mary). I used to write a monthly column on law for the banking magazine which was the flagship publication of the publisher where I worked. This elderly lady would appear crow-like on my floor shouting: 'Where's the lawyer? Where's the lawyer?', and waving my copy in her hand. It was covered in red ink. She required me to be extremely accurate, very pithy and clear enough that a child could grasp it. She gave me a priceless education.

I now have an editor all to myself. You would have thought that after thirty years I wouldn't need one. But I do. All writers do. It's no good seeking their comments then rejecting them. I used to do this with my editor.

'No, no, you don't understand,' I'd say, 'what I was trying to do was this.'

To which the obvious answer is: 'Well, why didn't you then? It's no good your piece requiring an oral accompanying explanation.'

These are typical writer / editor exchanges. I used to be guilty of these too. Then one day I realised that my editor was only trying to help me look better than I actually was. And that I shouldn't take it personally. That changed everything for me. I realised it was a waste of time.

So I don't argue any more. The sooner I do what my editor says the better. It means we can just get on to the next point, and the next, and the next, all of which will make my piece much better and me look a much better writer than I actually am.

Learn not to care

In fact, the more you write the less strongly you feel about your own style. I don't know any serious writer who likes re-reading what they've written after it's been published. No matter that you were happy with it when it went to press (you wouldn't have sent it if you weren't) it never reads as well later. Anyone who's satisfied with the way they write isn't going to strive to get better.

I once interviewed a young journalist for a position on a magazine I was editing (this one was about global investment management). He confessed to me that there was nothing he liked better of an evening than getting out his old cuttings (pieces of his that had been published) and poring over them. I didn't hire him.

You never become a good writer. You just reach a point where people are prepared to put up with what you've written. This is part of the humility you need to adopt as a writer. Anyone who reads what you've written is entitled to an opinion about it. Why else let them read it? I don't mind if people criticise my writing because I'm at the head of the queue. I dislike what I write more than anyone else does.

Professionals are told they should always seek feedback from clients after they've done a job. This is good advice. Clients are usually delighted to be asked and you can find out things about your service that are easy to improve yet will make a big difference to the client experience. But professionals are reluctant to do this.

It took me a long time to figure out why. It's because the client / adviser relationship is so personal that if you ask for feedback you're inviting personal criticism, and no one likes to do that. Especially not professionals. We're a thin-skinned lot, deeply insecure and compensate for that by appearing arrogant.

Yet those few professionals who do this – who do seek feedback – find very quickly that they don't take it personally. The more you do it the more it's water off a duck's back: you take the criticism for what it is – constructive, meant kindly, to enable you to keep the client and maybe get even more work from them. It's far better hearing that from the client than finding out later when they said nothing that they then defected to a competitor without your knowing.

And that's how I view criticism of my writing. It's not a criticism of me as a person, just me as a writer. And since that's part of what I do professionally, I'm always looking to improve it, to improve the user experience.

This does two things. It develops the humility that clients like. And it enables you to improve. You've cast off those shackles of amour propre (self love, as the French so beautifully put it). As one of my lawyer colleagues says: 'We're just builders, really, upmarket builders.' Well, yes, if only we were that good.

As soon as you switch into this mindset everything changes. The writing is here to serve a purpose, to help the reader / client. Everything else is subservient to this aim. The writing just becomes a means to an end, just part of what we need to be good at, to do well, in order to succeed in our chosen calling.

So my best advice to you is to get an editor. I did. It turned me into a best-selling author. You don't need one full-time: a colleague at work who'll look over your stuff and for whom you can do the same. Not for everything you write at work. Some things may be confidential and others not worth it – although I do get my editor, who happens to be a work colleague, to read even a three-line email before I press Send (more on emails later). But there should always be one or two people around at your level to whom you can show what you are doing.

Cut the purple passages

One of the things that invariably happens when your piece is edited is that the best bit gets cut. The bit that you like the most, worked longest on and encapsulates the whole piece is the one that any reader or editor will tell you to change.

I learnt this the hard way as a journalist. You write a piece and in it there is a paragraph that you are especially proud of, mainly because of the way you have written it. Inexplicably the subs (sub-editors) cut it out. Or you're 50 words over the wordcount and your piece needs to be cut to fit. Guess what? The best bit goes.

In fiction writing it's known as cutting purple passages. As Elmore Leonard said, 'If it reads like writing I leave it out.' Once you become experienced as a writer or editor you learn to chop these bits out yourself. And when you do the funny thing is that what's left is invariably stronger.

Re-imagine what you have written

A core skill as a writer is to be able to re-imagine what you have written. Because I am an editor first and foremost, my own editor says my key skill is in being able to rewrite a piece of mine over and over again in many different ways. To do this you need to stop caring about your style and care more about how best to get across what you are trying to say.

That's another reason for not labouring for hours on a first draft and ending up by thinking: there, that is perfect, that is the only way this can be said. Because you will not be able to come back to it and change it. And you need to be ready to change what you have written if you are going to improve it in any way.

This is the point Todd was making about Kidder. Experienced professional writers have a golden rule: write first, worry about it after. What they mean is: write something, anything, rather than nothing at all. Get something down on paper. Because once you've got something, anything down, you've got something to work with, something to edit, something to mull over and return to later. So the golden rule is: get it down first; then hack it about later.

Be an editor yourself

You'll learn a lot from editing what others have written. The trick, if you're acting as an editor for someone else, is to start editing as you start reading. Don't read it through once to get the feel of the thing then go back again to edit it in earnest.

Start making changes from the moment you start to read. This is because a reader will only read it once too. I had always instinctively worked this way as an editor before I read Gardner Botsford's memoir. He confirmed it. Botsford edited the *New Yorker*, a bastion of good writing, and he said (in his memoir *A Life Of Privilege, Mostly*) you should not read a piece through before editing it. In his view reading it through before starting to edit it attuned you to the writer's style and made you more accepting of it, whereas a reader would not show that degree of tolerance since they would at best read it once only if at all.

Invariably I find I make the most marks to a piece early on. I want the writer to get straight to the point. Once I've made those necessary initial changes to tell the reader what it's about and why it matters now (in other words to draw him in) the rest of the copy tends to fall into place quite easily. What this shows (again) is that good writing is about getting your thoughts in order (in an order that suits the reader). Once you do that the language tends to look after itself.

Be prepared to take time

There is a problem with all of this. It takes time. It takes time to write a second draft. It takes time to get someone else to read it and take in their comments and to learn to bite your tongue when they point out the piece's faults. This takes time, and people don't have time. No one has time any more.

This is true, of course. But the counter argument (sorry, this isn't an essay) is: why should the reader use their time to read anything you have written if you haven't taken the time to make it read as effectively as possible? If you can't be bothered to invest the time as writer, why should the reader?

The answer is that the more time and trouble you take the better and quicker you get. Everything I set out in this book will take you time to act upon. It will take more time than you are spending now. But as the principles become embedded in your approach, you will automatically start to write in the right way. You become a better writer. Your first drafts get better and better. In time – and it does take time, I don't deny that – you start to write what readers want to read.

This is not a counsel of perfection. You do what is optimal. You invest the least amount of time for the most benefit appropriate to the importance of the job in hand. And all the time you're getting better and faster. Once you have mastered these basic rules and made them second nature your first drafts will start to be close to the finished product.

Stephen Covey, famous for his book *The Seven Habits Of Highly Effective People*, talks about investing time in the short term for long term benefit. He says that delegating work to a junior colleague often takes a lot of time up front to get them trained to do what you need them to do. It is always tempting, instead, to do the work yourself. It will always be quicker. But, he says, stick with delegation. It may cost you time initially but, over time, it will save you time. That initial investment will be repaid many times over when your junior is able to take a task and do it from start to finish exactly as you would wish. That's where an enormous saving of time will occur.

So with writing. The initial investment of time will outweigh the immediate benefits. But in the long run you will learn to write so well that you will do so intuitively. I don't mean you'll be a Hemingway. But you will be good enough for work purposes. Your writing will be clearer and your analytical skills will be more obvious. It won't do your career any harm at all.

Mark Twain is said to have written to a friend: 'I'm sorry this letter is so long. I didn't have time to make it shorter.' It's a bit odd because, generally speaking, you want letters from friends to be as long as possible so you can get as much of them as possible. But in a business context his comment is spot on. It takes longer to write a short, comprehensive memo than it does a long one. It takes time to edit it down and to compress it so it still makes perfect sense but is a quicker and easier read. If you want your readers to spend their time reading what you have written it's your job to take the time to make it as easy and quick for them as possible – which is what we look at next.

CHAPTER 4

GET TO THE POINT

Knowing what you want to say and saying it as succinctly as possible - don't snag the reader's eye – use short words – Anglo-Saxon – Latin roots – monosyllables – short sentences – preferably with a verb – active not passive – short paragraphs – cut adjectives and adverbs – concentrate the action in the verb – use positives not negatives – avoid nominalisations – write like a journalist – say up front what it's about – Ricardo Semler – headline – no more than a side of A4 – tell someone what it's about and use that as your opening – be aware of house style – the two key journalistic principles – readers won't read your piece more than once – they will stop as soon as they can – pyramid – read it out loud – don't throttle the reader – how to stop

Finally. At long last. Isn't this where we should have started?

Getting to the point is about knowing what you want to say (which we looked at in the last chapter) then saying it as simply and quickly as possible (this chapter).

Don't snag the reader's eye

This is about using simple words and simple sentences. Why? Because we don't want to snag the reader's eye. Long words and complex constructs slow the reader down (the words 'complex constructs' are a case in point: I bet you stumbled over them, not least since constructs is usually a verb and here it is a strange noun used, even more strangely, in the plural; anyway, you get my point). If good writing is quick and clear it has to be simple.

Use short words

Whether you were taught to read individual letters or identify shapes of words, the fewer letters a word contains the quicker you'll be able to process what it is. Longer words have Latin roots. Short words tend to be Anglo-Saxon in origin. My favourite is 'get'. At school I was taught never to use it. Now I use it whenever I can. Get me.

Notice anything about the title of this book? Here it is:

> Get to the point: how to write well at work

They are all short words, every single one of 'em. Each is a monosyllable. That means it has a single stress. It's like a single note. 'One' is a monosyllable. The word 'single' has two syllables. The word 'monosyllable' has five. I could have called this book:

> Arriving at the message: a methodology supporting effective written communication in the workplace

But I didn't. The first line of a poem about a storm by the famous poet Ted Hughes reads: 'This house has been far out at sea all night' (from *Wind* about a storm in the night). Every word is a monosyllable.

Short words are the words of speech. They are natural. They are quick. They have movement (hence the line by Ted Hughes). They are easier to spell because they are shorter. They don't have obscure meanings the way longer ones tend to. And – most important of all – they are easier to read. They get the point across.

For anyone who thinks I'm dumbing down, George Orwell in his famous essay on language called *Politics And The English Language* wrote that you should use short words instead of long words and leave out words if you could do so.

Winston Churchill said: 'Short words are best' using short words to do so.

Mark Twain said that you should never use a five dollar word where a fifty-cent one would do (a slightly fancy way of making the same point). He also said you should delete every third word as a matter of course (he was only half-joking).

Use short sentences

A sentence has at heart a subject (doer), verb (action word) and object (something or someone done to). The cat sat on the mat.

This structure lends itself to rapid reading: who did what to whom. Not all sentences have this structure. Where they become particularly extenuated it's because they have subsidiary clauses: the cat, which was black, sat on the mat.

This disturbs the narrative drive. The reader has to come off on a subsidiary line of thought (the cat was black) before returning to the main point: the cat sitting on the mat. Better to say: the black cat sat on the mat.

Better still to leave it out altogether unless it's important. And if it's that important it probably merits a sentence to itself. The cat was black. It sat on the mat.

The original sentence conflates two ideas: the cat being black and sitting on the mat. This makes it harder to digest quickly.

It's traditional to write sentences with verbs. Older people may expect it. So do it until you know they don't. (Many of my sentences don't have verbs. This is bad English. But it is more conversational. It sounds more like me speaking. This apparently is what my readers like about my books. It's the books' style. At least, that's what my editor says. So I do it because that's what my readers want. But don't do it yourself unless and until you know yours do too. Many won't.)

Use the active not passive

The sentence we've just been looking at (the cat sat on the mat) is active. The mat was sat on by the cat is the passive version. You'd be surprised how often professionals use the passive. The resolution was passed by the board (the board passed the resolution). It has come to our attention (we have noticed).

There are times when the passive is appropriate, for instance when you don't want to be clear about how something happened (for instance, a lawyer writing about liability). But too often professional people default to the passive. Don't.

Use short paragraphs

The rule is that each paragraph should (like a short story) have a beginning, middle and end. The first sentence should set out the single theme the paragraph contains. I don't always follow this rule. I create paragraphs driven partly by what looks good on the page. We come back to how a piece of writing looks in the chapter after next.

Cut adjectives and adverbs

Adverbs (the cat sat on the mat drowsily) like adjectives (the black cat) slow sentences down. They get between the subject / verb / object construction.

With adjectives, we saw it's best to cut them or, if they are really necessary, to consider using a separate sentence to explain why.

With adverbs, choose an action word (verb) that also conveys the adverb (the cat drowsed on the mat) or, again, use a separate sentence.

Adjectives and adverbs are more often associated with fiction than workplace writing. But creative writing teachers will tell you to avoid them in fiction too. The best thriller writers keep them to a minimum to keep the story flowing. That works for us here.

Concentrate the action in the verb

If you cut out adverbs the action gets concentrated in the verb. Have you noticed how protagonists in newspaper stories tend to do things with a degree of violence or panache? The opposition **slams** government proposals. England **trounces** Australia at cricket. X **rejects** Y's plan.

These have become clichés and, Orwell said, should be avoided for that reason. A cliché is a word or expression that through over-use has lost its impact. But newspapers don't care about that: they want to get the point across quickly.

The same probably applies in business too. We're not writing fiction or great literature.

Use positives not negatives

This is like using actives rather than passives. Be positive rather than negative (there are a lot of Don'ts in this chapter. Sorry).

'Don't drop that cup' is a negative. It's telling you not to do something. It's a typical command from a parent to a toddler. You hear it all the time. Don't do this. Don't do that. But negatives are harder to grasp. You have to work out what the doing thing is (dropping) and then work out that you are not to do it (don't drop).

The toddler has to think: What is the doing word? Drop…

… and will have dropped the cup before its brain says: Now, don't do that dropping thing.

Result: cup on ground; angry parent; crying kid.

As with children so with readers. Tell them what to do, not what not to do.

Now, having said that, I'm going to break my own rule and write another negative rather than a positive.

Don't turn verbs into nouns

This is a bit more complex. Cat and mat are nouns. Turning a verb into a noun is called nominalisation (you can tell from its length and unreadability that it's a bad thing). In the book's title I said 'how to write well' not 'effective written communication'. Communication is a nominalisation. It is a noun converted from a verb (to communicate). Nominalisations kill off sentences. They turn them into sludge. They are no longer verbs (action words) and they tend to be longer which means they are slow.

Write like a journalist

What? You must be kidding. I'm a professional, not a tabloid hack.

Let me rephrase that: do what newspapers do. The key people at newspapers, who determine how they use language, are sub-editors, also known as copy editors (copy is newspaper-speak for text). They tend to be extremely knowledgeable about language and meticulous in its use.

The Sun newspaper is not known for its use of complex language (it takes all of the rules mentioned above to extremes) but it delivers exactly what its readers want: short words with a bit of humour. Stories tend to be strung through with puns. These are the work of the subs. The headlines are eye-catching. The two most famous are *Gotcha!* after the sinking of an Argentine battleship in the Falklands War in 1982 and *Freddie Starr ate my hamster*. These were the work of subs.

Newspapers excel in one thing: getting the point across as quickly as possible. This isn't always the case. Columns, features, magazine pieces, reviews – many of these can meander. But for news stories, yes.

Tell your reader up front what it's about

All news stories follow the same structure. A news story has a headline. Each successive sentence and paragraph expands upon that headline.

The closer you get to this model the better your writing will be.

If you want proof, ask Ricardo Semler.

Semler is the owner of Brazil's biggest and most successful steel company (at least he was when he wrote his book *Maverick* from which this comes). Semler inherited the business from his father but set about running it in a completely new way that transformed its fortunes. Investment banks and management consultants flocked to Semco to see how it was done.

One of his rules is: all memos have to have a headline. As he says, you are in no doubt what a memo's message will be if its heading is:

NEW SMELTING PROCESS WILL SAVE $200 MILLION

Semler also requires all memos to be no longer than one side of A4. That's about thirty lines or three hundred words. You can say whatever you need to about anything in that.

In *Maverick* Semler tells how he commissioned a report from a new senior employee, an ex-banker as it happened, into whether Semco should acquire another business. The report was lengthy with a lot of data presented in colourful tables and charts. The executive summary (the bit at the beginning, usually set out in a box, containing a list of the main findings or recommendations) said the proposed acquisition was a bad idea.

Semler read the executive summary with the ex-banker senior manager sitting there in front of his desk, then tossed the entire report – which had taken six months to produce – into the bin.

The senior manager was shocked.

'I agree with you,' Semler said. 'You think it's a bad idea and you've obviously done the research' – he thumbed through the pages of charts and tables – 'so we won't proceed.' He tossed the report into the bin exactly as you would a used newspaper. The report had done its job. The work that had led up to it wasn't wasted. Nor was the report itself. It helped the ex-banker formulate his own thinking. Which is what Semler was really interested in. He didn't need to read a long report to ascertain that.

So how do you start? How do you say up front what it's about?

Tell someone

My tip here is to tell a friend or colleague. Say: 'I have to write something at work and it's about…..' and then get him or her to write down what you say.

That's your opening sentence. It may not remain the opening sentence in the finished note (you'll no doubt come back and edit it later) but it's good enough to get you going. And if you do revise it later it's because it's got you to a place where you can see why you don't need it any more.

This also means that you put the most important information up front. You don't save it for the end or for later to make an impact. You say it right up front. I bet you that the smelting memo started off something like: 'If this company does not invest in new equipment we will be bust in five years' time.' That's a big deal. That's not a 'Oh, and by the way' point.

Be aware of house style

Now you may not be able to go this far. Every organisation has its own rules on how you set documents out. This is called house style. It comprises rules on how documents should look, standard headings, fonts (typefaces and sizes) and so on. It's part of an organisation's image and branding. You can't subvert it.

So you may not be able to use a headline. But you can probably use a subject line (as in an email) or adopt what would have been your headline as the opening sentence: 'This memo proposes adopting a new smelting process that will save us $200 million.'

Semco uses headlines because it was Semler's idea and it's his company. But I still think there is more room to exploit an organisation's house style creatively than people think. I don't recommend spending hours on it. But just doing small things that might help without contravening the rules. We'll look at some of these ideas in the chapter after next.

The two key journalistic principles

Now I want to turn to the key principles that flow from the way newspapers are written and which are absolutely germane to business writing. They are:

- Readers won't read your piece more than once.
- Readers will stop as soon as they can and are unlikely to reach the end.

Readers won't read it more than once and they are unlikely to read it to the end. Readers want to stop reading as soon as they can. And once they stop they won't go back to it – another reason for keeping words and sentences short: if the reader's eye gets snared by complicated words (like complicated) and extended sentence constructions they may stop reading then and there, never to return. It's the point about snagging the reader's eye I made earlier.

The journalistic style of writing is like a pyramid. Stories in newspapers are written in such a way that the reader can stop anywhere and still know what's happened. The headline encapsulates the entire story. Each sentence adds more information. Crucially, the reader can stop whenever he likes and still know what the story was about. The assumption is that the reader won't reach the end. This is what all readers in a business context want.

You can now see why I've been banging on about not having a conclusion. Readers either won't reach it or, if they do reach the end, it's because it's a quick read so they will remember what you said earlier anyway.

Take that *Sun* headline *Gotcha!* It came from the war with Argentina over the Falkland Islands in 1982. The British sank the Argentine battleship the Belgrano. *The Sun* newspaper's front page was a picture of the stricken warship going down with one word over the top: *Gotcha!* The picture and the word told everybody the story. It was a terrible tragedy and a lot of Argentine mariners died. I'm not mentioning it to glorify war or to take sides, but because in the context of conveying information it did the job.

All newspaper stories adopt this approach. They put the most important information first. Those who want to read on to get more detail can do so. Those who just need the headline can move on. Most people who work read newspapers (often on the way into work). They are used to consuming information this way.

How we take in information in our lives outside work has a big impact on how we take in information at work. We are all highly sophisticated ingesters of data. We have advertising stuff thrown at us all the time. We know to a nano-second when to read on and when to discard it. Why would you not deploy such finely-tuned skills at work too?

So use the same technique when you write for work. Be user friendly. Allow them to read at work in the same way as they do outside. They will like you for it.

Anyone can do it

What's great about all of this is that anyone can do it – and that's because keeping it simple is the key. You don't need to have had an expensive education to write well for work. In fact it can be a disadvantage. If you have been well educated and feel you can already write well, it is harder to accept that you have anything left to learn about it and harder to unlearn what you've been taught. But if you haven't been that fortunate you can still write well at work. I'm not saying it will be easy. I'm not saying it won't take time. But with a bit of time and effort you can do it.

And you can start today. You don't have to do anything big. Just start doing some of the things I have suggested and your writing will improve immediately – and so, crucially, will your confidence.

Anyone can be a good writer. Not a great one, necessarily. But a good one.

Read it out loud

A good test of the readability of your writing is reading it out loud. Really. Go into a room on your own and read the thing out loud. I do and I find myself stopping regularly to amend what I've written.

The reason this works is because almost all of us vocalise as we read, that is, as the words are transmitted to our brains we speak them to ourselves silently. Sometimes you see people moving their lips as they read. It's the same thing.

The only people who don't do this are those who've learnt how to speed-read. I've been taught to speed-read although I don't use it much myself. Speed-reading teaches you to scan down a page rather than across the page (it's why newspaper columns are narrow so the eye can go straight down rather than from side to side) and in order to skim quickly you have to stop vocalising. But most of us do.

Don't throttle the reader

Now, if that's the case it means that readers will effectively read your piece internally to themselves. So if you have a sentence that's too long readers will start to run out of mental oxygen. They will start to feel as if they are gasping for breath. I call this mental asphyxiation. It's as bad in reading as in real life.

So don't do this to your reader. Reading your piece out loud is a good way of testing sentence length. It will help you shorten phrases to make your piece faster. It also helps you identify and correct clumsy language.

For example, replace 'in the event of' with ' if' and 'at this moment' with 'now'. Replace 'in order to' with 'to' and so on. Any phrase that sounds clunky when you read it out loud will be clunky when the reader reads it.

Nowadays Macs and PCs will read it out to you. It might sound robotic but you can be making the amendments to the print-out as the computer reads it out.

Reading your piece out loud will help you avoid complex words you don't understand and sentence constructions that you're not sure are accurate (for instance plural subjects with singular verbs).

How to stop

If you don't need a conclusion, what do you do when you reach the end?

Answer: you stop.

Stopping dead sounds odd. When you first start to end your pieces this way it will feel odd. But when you go back and read them (aloud) it won't.

However, If that Is too sudden, you can say what the next steps are:

Once I have your thoughts on this and discussed it with X, Y and Z I will circulate a revised proposal.

Or you can end with (in marketing jargon) a call to action:

Please call me to discuss the implications for your business.

CHAPTER 5

DISMANTLE THE SCAFFOLDING

We read much faster than we write – we write as if it will take the reader as long to read – delete the connecting phrases – speed of eye-to-brain transmission (SEBT) – the brain makes logical connections – exploiting SEBT – *The Economist* – stringing data throughout a piece – limited repetition – mesmerising the reader – longer pieces like reports – executive summaries

The big idea in this chapter is that we read much faster than we write.

Obvious to say, but easily forgotten.

I'm a fast writer, but it still takes me about 15-20 minutes to think through and write a page in this book, and this is stuff I know about. But when you are writing about something new, complex or technical it will take you a lot longer, especially if it's for work.

To write a technical piece of advice for a client that is a page long could take you as long as an hour-and-a-half, even longer possibly.

I'm hoping it takes you no more than five minutes to read a page in this book. It will take a client a few minutes more than that to read a page of advice. But certainly not as long as it took you to write.

In fact the better written it is, the longer it will have taken you to write and the less time it will take the client to read.

So we need to write in the knowledge that the reader will read what we have written (if at all) at a speed that is a fraction of the time it has taken us to write.

But we don't.

We automatically write as if the reader will take as long to read as we do to write.

That's why we put in so much connecting clutter.

As we write we make allowances for the reader. It's as if the reader is a sniffer dog following in our tracks and we have to put out little tidbits to keep the reader on the trail. So we use phrases such as:

- It follows that…
- You can see from the above that…
- As mentioned earlier…
- To conclude…

We do this to keep the reader reading, to act as little signposts along the way. Delete them all, every single one of them. They slow your writing down, make it turgid and encourage readers to stop.

I know it follows that. I know because you have been leading me down a well-thought-through and logical argument.

I can see from the above because I was up there only a minute ago.

I know you mentioned it earlier. I read it two minutes ago.

You don't need to conclude. You've already told me and I can see from the page that there are only two lines to go (both of which are probably unnecessary anyway).

These connecting phrases are what I call the scaffolding. You may feel the need to put them in as you are constructing your piece. But you equally need to take them out before you send the piece out to the client. All they do is get in the way. They slow your piece down.

A challenge

I challenge you to take out a piece you have recently written and cross out all the connecting clutter, the scaffolding as I call it, the joints and frames we put in while we're building our piece. And while you're about it don't forget to take that thing headed 'conclusion' and make it the opening paragraph (as I've already suggested you do).

Now tell me the piece isn't a hundred times better. It's a quicker, punchier read.

This is the start of something altogether more exciting. It's what I call the Speed of Eye-to-Brain Transmission (SEBT). What this means is that we can trust that the reader's brain will make most of the connections for us.

Exploiting SEBT

I've already said we read fast. What happens is that the eye scans the page and relays the words to the brain. The brain turns them into thought. It does this as fast as a computer. It is able to do so because of two things:

- It assumes a logical connection between what follows and what came before.
- Even if there isn't one it will process the information as if there were.

Good business writers exploit SEBT and turn this to their advantage.

For example, there may be three reasons why a course of action is recommended. You and I would say exactly that: 'There are three reasons why...' and we would probably set them out as a bulleted list.

Writers who are aware of SEBT don't do that. They don't bother to say there are three. They just say what they are. The reader's brain will work out there are three. For this reason the words 'of two things' before the two bullets above are redundant. Your brain would have worked out that there were two reasons, helped by the layout (the two bulleted points).

Or take the following example:

> There are three reasons why we need to dismantle the scaffolding of what we write. First, people read more quickly than they write so they don't need so much signposting. Second, removing it accelerates the flow of our writing. Third, it's unnecessary because the brain assumes a logical sequence between sentences so will make the necessary connections anyway.

Now, try this:

> *We need to dismantle the scaffolding of what we write. People read more quickly than they write so they don't need it. Removing it accelerates the flow of our writing. The brain will make the necessary connections anyway.*

It's not a great example and you could argue that the edited version makes more sense than it should because you've just read the longer version. But the principle holds good.

A publication that does this regularly is *The Economist* newspaper. It has more layers of sub-editing than any other newsstand publication. A piece written by a journalist will be edited by half-a-dozen others before it goes to print. A lot of that editing is taking stuff out to make it more concise and a lot of that editing is premised on SEBT.

In fact a lot of what I am telling you – as in the last chapter – comes from journalism. Newspapers were expert at giving readers what they wanted. The same types of story appeared in the same places (politics near the front, sports at the back) so people could start where they knew what they wanted would be. Headlines were designed to be scanned so you knew immediately if you wanted to read on. Stories were written so you could stop anywhere and certainly didn't have to read to the end (I mentioned *Gotcha!* in the last chapter).

They also did something else. Editors knew that what fascinates humans most is other humans. People are interested in people. They want to see them (hence photos) and want to read about them. So every newspaper piece will always tell you a person's name, marital status, age, livelihood and place of residence. But – crucially – this is not lumped together in one sentence:

> *Joe Boyd is 51, a plumber and lives in Harlow with his wife and three children.*

This sentence stops the story dead in its tracks. It describes Joe Boyd but does not advance the action. It does not keep us reading. These are incidental details that, when lumped together, stop the narrative drive and discourage us from reading on.

So what newspapers did was to string this information throughout the piece.

> *Joe Boyd, a plumber, was stopped by police on Wednesday night. Boyd, 51, was wrongly mistaken for Jack Prentice, recently escaped from Pentonville prison. Boyd, who is from Harlow, was held for twelve hours. He said it was a terrifying ordeal. Boyd, who is married with three children, said he was considering bringing a claim for wrongful arrest.*

Writers who grasp this use it to seed apparently unconnected pieces of data throughout their piece, accelerating the flow and ensuring the reader keeps reading, relying on SEBT to keep the reader pressing on even in the face of this apparent discontinuity.

Where I have seen this used to greatest effect is in highly technical and complex writing. For example, a typical legal piece involves analysing a court decision. It will set out the facts, the arguments the two parties used, what the trial judge decided and why. Then, because complex cases which make new law are usually appealed, what the appeal court said and why it differed from what the trial judge said.

Bored, aren't you? That's because this order is chronological (chronos = Greek for time: the order in which things happened). It doesn't say which arguments won the day and how the trial and appellate courts treated them. (By the way, there's a point here about story-telling. Some people like recounting information by telling a chronological story around it – 'then she did this and he said that'. But in business this is a no-no. People want to get straight to the point. They want to know the end before the intervening steps that got there.)

Mesmerising the reader

I once read a piece about a court case that I couldn't put down. And that's because the writer (a lawyer) completely disregarded the chronology of the case. Instead he looked at the arguments and as he went through he slipped in all the incidental information about the facts and what the trial judge decided and what the appellate court then said (the incidental information you need to know, but which holds the story up).

And when I came to analyse why his piece had been so compelling I realised that he had used this technique of stringing information throughout the piece at times when it made no logical sense for that information to be there at all. He knew the reader's brain could take it – that it would concentrate on the arguments but assimilate these other facts as it went along. That way his piece stayed quick and held the reader's attention throughout. The reader's brain would forgive the writer illogicality in return for the speed.

What's more, by doing this he could throw in much more detail about how good the arguments themselves actually were. His piece came to life. It lived and breathed. It moved sinuously from side to side like a snake. It was mesmerising. You want your pieces to move like snakes. You want them to dance, to mesmerise.

And – the greatest compliment I can pay him – it meant his piece could be read and enjoyed by non-lawyers alike, by real people, and not just people like him and me, and hold their attention.

This is advanced writing and not to be attempted until you really know what you are doing.

Limited repetition

What follows is controversial. If I am right that people will only read your piece once and may not get to the end, then I believe limited repetition is OK. What I mean by this is that if what you are trying to say or explain is complex, it may be worth doing it in more than one way so the reader gets it.

There is an analogy here with double negatives. 'I didn't do it to no one' is ungrammatical. But these constructions were perfectly all right a few hundred years ago. What they do, in an oral tradition, is drive the point home. You're only going to hear it once. It leaves you in no doubt.

Once things got written down people could go over them more than once and became a bit snobbier about the language used (since only the rich, being educated, could write).

But nowadays, since readers don't treat the written word with the same deference as of yore, you may need to use some of those old techniques to ram a point home. I don't mean saying the same thing twice using the same language. I mean finding different ways to express it. This becomes more relevant the longer your piece is.

Longer pieces like reports

Some writers suggest that if you are writing a long piece you need to signpost the reader the way: tell him at the start what you will be covering; then along the way tell him where you are at each stage; and (no doubt) tell him at the end where you've been.

I'm not sure I agree. I think that if you just get on and say what you want to say then it becomes a shorter and faster experience for the reader anyway, without the need for this additional signposting. If it's a really long report then it's customary to use an executive summary. This is usually the highlights set out as a series of bullet points right at the start of the report, often in a box. What you are doing is using a visual signpost, helping the reader by the way the words look on the page.

This visual signposting is what we look at next.

CHAPTER 6

SPACE MATTERS

How a piece looks matters – house style – short paragraphs – Lord Denning – breaking up the text – numbered paragraphs – bulleted lists – emboldening – sub-heads and cross-heads – frequently asked questions – writing your piece as a slide deck – using boxes – tint of black – how look changes meaning – always read your piece in hard copy – no footnotes (again)

It's odd that a book on writing should spend any time on the space around the words. But how a piece of writing looks matters. A solid block of text is uninviting and puts the reader off. Breaking the same piece up into short paragraphs with headings (called cross-heads or sub-heads – head is short for heading) makes it far more welcoming to the eye. Making it look different somehow makes it read differently.

Supposing the Introduction had looked like this:

> This book could change your life. It's ridiculous but it's true. And that's because one of the biggest things preventing young people from getting the job they want or being successful in a role is the way they write. At work the way you write is at the heart of the way you communicate. In the workplace you will do more communicating by writing than anything else: emails, memos, reports, even letters. It far outweighs the number of times you will speak memorably in a meeting or on the phone. It will endure for longer too. In fact later on in this book I tell you to assume your emails will last for ever and be read by everyone. Even if you do presentations, how you write them (which includes how you structure them) will determine their success even more than the way in which you deliver them. Great delivery with poor content is still a poor presentation. Great content poorly delivered will still provide some value (although of course you want to do both well: both the writing and the delivery; this book is about the writing). How you write is visible to everyone, your boss and clients alike. So this book is aimed at young professionals just starting out on their careers, who know they need to write well but aren't sure how to do it. And why should you listen to me? I'm a professional (a lawyer, who has also been a management consultant and held various senior roles in law firms heading up marketing, training and knowledge management). I'm a professional writer who writes books like this that people praise for their clarity. I'm also a teacher and trainer. I have a PGCE, taught for ten years on an MBA and train professional people in how to write. Crucially and unusually for someone in a professional role, I've been a journalist and editor. That's where I learnt what I know about writing. It wasn't from being a lawyer.

It looks deeply uninviting and impenetrable, like coming up against a sheer cliff-face. You have to steel yourself to begin to read it, that's if you bother to at all.

Even this page looks grim because we haven't had one of those cross-heads yet. So I'm going to put one in.

How words look on the page matters

Now, whether you can use space as you would like will depend on the house style of the organisation you're in (house style is something I mentioned earlier). So you may not have much freedom to do what I'm about to say.

But even the most restrictive house style will allow room for some visual impact.

For example, you can use short paragraphs (like the previous few). They will allow more white space on to the page. The standard rule is that each paragraph should contain a single idea or argument. But, more importantly I think, each paragraph should allow the reader a chance to pause a moment for breath.

Short paragraphs are like exclamation marks – they can be visually striking, especially if they are just one sentence long. But too many short paragraphs in succession can ruin the effect. A judge famous to lawyers was Lord Denning. He was famous because, apart from being an iconoclast who changed the law at every opportunity, he wrote his judgments in short sentences and paragraphs. This was highly refreshing for law students. But sometimes he wrote too many short sentences in a row. It can have the same staccato effect as a piledriver. It gives you a headache.

Breaking up the text

If you're writing a report you may want to use numbered paragraphs for ease of reference when people respond.

When setting out a list set it out as a succession of bullets, not as narrative.

The reasons for using a bulleted list are that it is:

- Eye-catching
- Easier to scan down
- A visual indication of how many items there are

By contrast, a narrative list: is not as visually striking; has its own accepted punctuation (using semi-colons – we'll come to this later); and looks a lot denser to disentangle on the page.

You'll see I've set out the arguments as a bulleted list and then as a narrative list to make the point.

Emboldening the first few words of a paragraph (as here) can be effective. It catches the eye and may enable you to comply with your organisation's house style. If you do this at strategically important points in your piece the effect can be disproportionately greater than a few words in bold would suggest.

Another way is to use sub-heads and cross-heads (like this)

Generally you'll want to use them to signpost a new topic or theme or section in the piece. In newspapers they aren't used in this rigorous way. Often a sub-head in a newspaper has little to do with the logical order of the story. They are actually used to break up columns of text and, if a story is a bit short, take up space so the text falls neatly to the bottom of the page. If you look carefully I do a bit of that in this book, driven as much by the look of the page as the content itself.

In general, the longer the piece the more you may need to break it up visually (see box opposite).

Frequently Asked Questions

A fast way of getting information across is through FAQs (Frequently Asked Questions).

How do FAQs work? You set out a series of questions and answers that cover what most readers want to know.

Why are they good? The reader can quickly skim down to the question(s) relevant to him or her.

Are there any drawbacks? FAQs can appear a little impersonal (as if they are generic answers for everyman) and so make your writing seem less involving. However, they are better than rhetorical questions. A rhetorical question, so called because it is a device of rhetoric (oratory or speech-making), is one that the speaker asks just to be able to answer it. Purists say that you shouldn't ask questions just to answer them. Why do they say that? Because in journalism it's regarded as a lazy way of raising an issue (there, 'Why do they say that?' was the rhetorical question). FAQs aren't rhetorical questions in my view and, if they are the most direct way of getting information across, use them. Better still, put your FAQs in a box.

The real message of boxed copy and FAQs is that visuals are more eye-catching than words. This is a book about writing but pictures are more powerful than words: they can impart a message more directly and quickly.

Think about whether any of your content can be delivered visually, say through a flow diagram (if it's a process) or a pie or bar chart if it is statistical. Even a pie chart with just three segments conveys that information more directly than the equivalent in words. A more visual way of using words is via a slide deck.

Writing your piece as a slide deck

People like presentations instead of reports. They prefer someone talking to them rather than reading something that could be turgid and poorly written.

For this reason more people in the workplace are using slide decks instead of reports. I do this myself. It depends entirely on what the audience wants.

The traditional way of doing this is by bullets (no more than five or six) per slide. But a long presentation consisting solely of slides made up entirely of bullets can be boring (it's known as Death By PowerPoint – PowerPoint being the Microsoft app). People are much readier to experiment with pictures and video – but that takes us into the realms of presentations and away from writing, which is the focus of this book. I don't discuss it here. But I approve.

Using boxes

Possibly the most useful tip I learnt as an editor was about boxing off text.

Boxes are a good way of separating off copy (text) you need to include but which would otherwise hold up the main narrative thrust or break the flow.

In magazines they are often used to frame a subsidiary story or something that is interesting but not central – which is why in the US they are called sidebars. So, for example, an involved technical term or formula could merit a **(see box)** when it's first mentioned in the text and the box could be headed with that term for easy cross-reference.

Anything in boxes (especially if the box has a light grey tint, such as 10% of black) is eye-catching to a disproportionate effect.

The other use of boxes is to give prominence to the take-away: if there is a set of points you want the reader to go away with (the take-away) you can list these in a box. Here you use the box to give the most important aspects additional prominence.

This is what makes boxed copy so versatile. Boxes work particularly well for executive summaries.

If you have room (and house style allows) to give a box a heading (as here) so much better.

What I want to know is – and try to be honest – was this box the first thing your eye went to on this double-page spread? I bet it was. Our eye is drawn to anything visual.

How look changes meaning

Always print out what you write. How the words look on the page will be different from how they look on screen. You will find yourself changing what you have written even though you may have been perfectly happy with it on screen. I don't know why this is, but it happens every time.

Even if you've printed it out at an interim stage, always print out the final version and read it through (preferably fresh – circadian rhythms) in hard copy form before sending it off. Don't just rely on spellcheck. You will always see mistakes you didn't see on screen.

Just pausing here for a moment, compare the look of this chapter with previous ones. It looks more interesting, doesn't it, even before you start reading it? That's because of the layout. However, it also looks a mess because in order to give you examples of different styles I have (deliberately) avoided the sort of consistency that a house style imposes.

One other point about the look of the thing. If you are writing an email, keep it short. There's nothing worse (particularly on a mobile device) than opening a long email. Try to ensure the reader does not have to scroll down. But I'm getting ahead of myself. Email is what we move on to next.

One final point.[1]

---

[1] No footnotes. Ever. Unless you're writing an academic paper. If they contain important information, put it in the body of the text or an appendix. Otherwise they're just a distraction. They tempt the reader's eye away, possibly never to return. You see: you're down here now.

CHAPTER 7

EMAIL IS KRYPTONITE

Email could destroy your career – assume you are writing for everyone for ever – is a phone call better? – tone – salutation – sign off – set out like a letter – don't make the reader scroll – always spellcheck – print out longer emails – avoid recalling – send out a replacement – avoid humour – don't forward funny emails – don't reply in anger – decide how quickly to respond – whether to respond at all – don't just Reply All – check to the end of the string – make the subject line relevant – draft your email elsewhere until you are ready to send – be aware of formatting issues – always attach attachments – email is not txt – adopt the style of the sender

A lot of business writing these days is done by email. And here the rules are different. If anything email is even harder. And that's because it has the potential to destroy your career.

You are writing for everyone for ever

Email contains a paradox which is this: it seems ephemeral, like a text on a phone. You write it, send it and it disappears into the ether. Only it doesn't disappear. It remains on systems as a permanent record. And it can be forwarded to anyone.

So it can last for ever and be read by everyone.

But it beguiles you into forgetting this. So you treat it casually, press the wrong button or the right one but in haste and – bingo – career disaster. And if you try to recall it that just makes people even more eager to see what you said that you now want to take back. So recall never works.

Every so often there's a story of an email going viral. It's almost invariably something embarrassing. It often ends up with the originator being sacked. Consider how many emails end up being used as evidence in court cases. Think how your email might sound if read out in a court of law. That's the test.

When you are using email you are effectively broadcasting from the rooftop to the entire world, though you may not know it.

So, however quick and temporary the medium may feel, it is full of traps for the unwary. It is out to trick you.

So treat it with caution. It lasts for ever and is read by everyone. Remember that and you'll be fine.

Is a phone call better?

Email is actually a brilliant medium of communication. It can be quicker and easier than picking up the phone. It crosses time zones. You write it when you want and the reader can read it when she wants. You write it once and many people can receive it at the same time. It's superbly versatile.

But always ask yourself whether a phone call might be better. If the content is complex so will take a long time to write, or requires a discussion, then pick up the phone. Ask yourself what your reader wants: phone call or email?

And that's because the easiest mistake to make is one of tone.

Tone

Email has almost the same immediacy as the phone but without all of the surrounding messaging that comes through your voice. So it is very easy for the reader to think you are being abrupt or sarcastic when you're not.

It is much harder for a reader of an email to identify your tone of voice than if they are hearing you speak. Almost invariably emails are taken the wrong way. If they can be read to be abrupt, rude or sarcastic, they will be. If you use the reader's name (Hi Chris) and they reply without using yours (In response to your question, the answer is…) they may think you're being overly familiar. You may think they're being rude.

Emails can appear more formal than intended. They can also appear more informal than intended. One seems stuffy. The other may imply lack of respect.

Even the way you address the reader can be an issue. Do you say Dear Chris? Or Hi Chris? Or just Chris? What if you haven't met them before – is using their first name too informal? But is saying Mr Stoakes or Dear Mr Stoakes too stuffy? And how do you end? Just with your name? or Best wishes? Or Yours sincerely (sounds too much like a letter)?

I tend to use Hi [name] and sign off Kind regards. If the reader is older or more senior than me I might drop the Hi and just use their first name. Or just their surname prefaced with Mr or Ms.

Most people set emails out like letters. So you have the salutation (greeting) such as Hi Chris and then drop down a line and start a sentence. My own style is not to do that. I will say Hi [name] then insert a dash and continue on the same line with a lower case letter:

> Hi Max – yes, tomorrow for lunch is fine. Say 12.30? See you then.
>
> Kind regards
>
> Chris

I do this because it seems more immediate, more like talking. But there are times when you need to make it virtually the same as a letter. For instance, if you don't know the client then this may a safe starting point. You can then study the response and follow the client's lead.

Keep it short and don't make the reader scroll

Keep your email short, preferably no longer than the view in which it opens. I try to avoid making readers scroll down too much (especially if they are using a mobile device). They may print a long email off but then may not read it.

You may be better off attaching a document with a one-line covering email than setting it all out in the body of the email itself. However, there is always the risk that the attachment won't be read, especially if it's a one-to-many communication. So you may need to use the string and the email text to excite readers sufficiently to open the attachment.

Always spellcheck

However short the email, always spellcheck it. Almost invariably if your email contains a typo you will spot it just after you have pressed Send, no matter how many times you have already read it through.

Print out longer emails

You shouldn't be writing long emails anyway. But if you are, print them out and read them in hardcopy.

The reason for spellchecking – indeed, for any of these rules – is because the effort it takes to undo the consequences of an email that shouldn't have gone is huge in proportion to the time it takes to make sure it is completely correct before it goes out.

If you do have to undo an email one tip is to simply send out a replacement: 'Please discard the previous email and refer to this instead.' This achieves two things. First it corrects the wrong. Second it does so in a way that is almost off-hand (as if you're not really that bothered, so the transgression can't have been that bad) and in turn means recipients are less likely to bother to trawl through both comparing them in order to see where the first was wrong.

Don't be funny

I have a warning pasted to my monitor at work:

KEEP EMAILS SHORT – NO HUMOUR

One of the things that translates hardest to email is humour, even allowing for the fact that humour is very much a matter of personal taste. What might seem a funny quip can in the so-called cold light of day seem at best crass and at worst stupid. So avoid humour. The number of times I have penned a witty rejoinder then deleted it are legion. Increasingly I'll sleep on it. If it isn't as funny the next day, I delete it. It never is.

Don't join in others' humour. Don't forward funny emails

I'm sorry to be a killjoy but it is easy to get caught up in a humorous string (usually at a fellow employee's expense) and forward it on. This is how office jokes go viral and become global. Employers don't like it. By forwarding an email you can be implicated and, if it is defamatory, could be liable. Curb the temptation to join in.

If I see a funny cartoon I'll show it to a colleague rather than scan it and email it. Then it is less likely to be forwarded and you are less likely to be in breach of copyright or worse.

Don't reply in anger

It is as easy to misunderstand the intended tone of an email as it is to get it wrong when writing. So the risk of taking offence is high. You must curb the temptation to bang off an angry reply.

It's worth taking a leaf out of Neuro-Linguistic Programming: assume that people's strategies are pure but their execution is poor. In other words, always think the best of senders. Don't assume they want to irritate or offend you. And, even if they did, take into account how they may be feeling. They may be having an off-day or allowing something bad in their life outside work to colour the way they behave in the office. In short, be forgiving.

By all means draft a reply to get it out of your system, but don't send it. Put it to one side, preferably overnight. Get a trusted colleague to look at the exchange (your editor?) and give you her thoughts. And even if she agrees with you, use your draft email as a script for a phone call, rather than sending it off. Phone calls don't leave the same trail.

Decide how quickly to respond

Email can set up an expectation of immediate response. You will only know over time what a client's expectations are (you could do a lot worse than ask them). Sometimes you should send an immediate acknowledgement with a timeframe for when a fuller reply can be expected – in which case make sure you do meet that further deadline, otherwise the client will be disappointed. You have set up an expectation that you need to meet.

In the days before email we had faxes (facsimiles – you put a letter into the fax machine and it popped out at the client's end a minute or two later, so it was almost as immediate). At the time I remember a boss of mine saying that he never replied immediately to a client's fax. He would sit on it for at least a day or two. I was stunned. Why? I asked. He explained: because otherwise the client might not feel you had given the issue the necessary care and consideration. And replying too quickly might make the client feel it wasn't a hard question so therefore wasn't worth a big fee. I'm not sure that would work now.

(It was this same boss who periodically emptied his in-tray into the bin. He explained that his PA put all the important stuff – anything to do with money or anything from a client – in a different, much smaller in-tray. This bigger one was for internal memos from elsewhere in the firm. These could be binned because, as he said, 'If it's important enough and I am a key stakeholder, someone will sooner or later come and see me about it.' So you can see how many obstacles there can be between your beautifully-crafted memo and its ultimate intended recipient.)

Decide whether to respond at all

It can be tricky with someone more senior to know whether to reply at all. I used to send acknowledgements as a matter of course, to show my boss I had received her instruction and was working on it. Then I realised that this was an unnecessary addition to her already-full inbox. She assumed the system had delivered her email and that I would respond when I had something meaningful to say. So I stopped doing it. It can be tricky knowing when someone specifically does not expect you to reply. Otherwise you can end up in an unnecessary continuation of an exchange that neither of you wants. Often a final line that says Have a good evening or Have a great weekend means that no reply is expected.

Don't just Reply All. Read to the end of the string

It is tempting just to send your reply to all of the people the previous message went to. But that's often not a good idea. Email is irritating. It's irritating to be copied in on emails that neither require your action nor are for your information.

But the biggest mistake is not reading to the end of the string before pressing Reply All. At the bottom of the string there may be information that not all recipients should see.

Worse (and I have seen this happen) there may be an unwise remark made about one of the recipients who wasn't previously copied in but now is and which comes to his attention once he is added to the string. If he happens to be a client it's a disaster.

At the very least consider deleting the rest of the string before pressing Send.

Make the subject line relevant

Equally irritating is when the subject line doesn't change to reflect the change in the exchange below. Some organisations use subject lines strictly to be able to file emails according to client and project. Check what the rules are in your place of work and follow them. The subject line is the headline. It can be a useful way of exciting interest in the contents of the email (remember Ricardo Semler). Think about how the exchange may develop and choose a subject line that is future-proofed.

Draft your email elsewhere until you're ready to send

This is a useful tip. With email the Send button is like the ring in *Lord Of The Rings*. It draws your finger like a magnet. Before you know it you have pressed it by accident and sent out an incomplete or unchecked email.

The way to avoid this is to draft your text in a fresh email then, when it's ready, go back to the original and paste your reply back in. This way there is no risk of the draft email going out prematurely or inadvertently if there are no names in the To and Cc boxes.

Be aware of formatting issues

Just be aware that on some systems if you edit an existing email or draft before forwarding or sending it, the font or formatting may change where the edit's been made. This looks bad and is revealing. What I do is draft my reply in Word and then drop the complete text into the email when it's finished, checked and ready to go.

Always attach attachments

It is incredibly easy to make this mistake: refer to an attachment then press Send before you've attached it. If you are going to attach a document then attach it to your email before you draft the email.

Email is not txt

Email is a substitute for a letter not for a text. So use proper spellings and proper sentences. Write as you would if you were drafting a note rather than if you were sending a text. In other words, err on the side of caution until you know what the recipient is happy with.

Adopt the style of the sender

This means you can't go wrong. Study the style, format and tone of the email you are responding to – even the length – and respond in kind.

CHAPTER 8

THINGS PEOPLE GET WRONG

The need to get grammar and spelling right – troublesome words – stationery – stationary – disinterested – anticipated – embarrassed – harassed – accommodation – practise – practice – licence – license – affect – effect – fewer – less – principal – principle – e.g. – i.e. – numbers – different – compared – all right – always – between – among – unique – criteria – data – who – whom – myself – me – I – hopefully – literally – important – being consistent – split infinitives – punctuation – apostrophes – brackets (parentheses) – quotation marks – semi-colons – colons – And and But at the start of sentences

There are some aspects of writing you have to get right. If you don't, readers will think you careless or stupid. I know. I agree with you. It's pathetic. But I said earlier that whatever the reader wants is right. And some are purists. They still judge people by these things. So we need to get these things right.

In professional life, getting grammar and spelling right is important. Professional people can be pedants because they feel they write correctly. They pride themselves on these things. Lawyers, in particular, are very keen on this. Give a lawyer a draft to review and the first thing he or she will do is to start amending the text. It's less of an obsession in other professions, but it still matters.

Clients can be pedants when it comes to language because it may be the only way they can tell whether their professional adviser is any good, unless they too understand that discipline. Besides, if a client is paying £10,000 for a piece of advice they will be less than impressed if the memorandum is ungrammatical or contains spelling mistakes or typos. It may make them doubt the validity of the advice.

Do what you know to be absolutely correct unless and until you know the reader will tolerate a more relaxed approach.

I happen to think that a lot of things about spelling and grammar are silly. Language is forever evolving and that's good. For example I like American spellings: color for colour; center for centre; thru for through; and so on. But for now over here we use Anglicised (English) spelling. So there we are. I happen to believe that texting and social media will have a massive impact on formal language and I welcome that. It will become more phonetic (spelling as it sounds): knife will become nife. Things like speech marks (inverted commas), apostrophes and semi-colons will disappear. They already look archaic and dated.

But for the time being you need to know the rules as they are now. The funny thing about grammar and spelling is that people get uptight about the smallest things. It's how Lynne Truss wrote a best seller about apostrophes. People take it personally (the way people take their own style seriously and don't like being criticised for it).

In this chapter I'm not going to give you a lesson in grammar. If you were that interested you would have read about it already and wouldn't be reading a book like this to learn about it. Besides, grammar isn't an end in itself. It's a set of rules so that the writer writes in a way the reader can read. I still believe that simplest is best. If you keep your writing simple a lot of the complex rules go away. They are just not relevant. Use short words in short, active sentences, ending with a stop. Then you can't go wrong.

No, instead I'm going to point out the big, common mistakes which I see regularly.

Words

So, let's start with words. I have a golden rule: if I encounter a word I don't know I always look it up. I keep a dictionary by my side to do so (as Mary did). I suggest you do the same or use a reliable online equivalent.

Stationery is the stuff you write on ('e' is for Envelope). **Stationary** means stopped ('a' for At rest or Arrested).

Disinterested means neutral (not taking sides). It does not mean uninterested which means bored.

Anticipated does not mean expected. It means doing something in advance of something else which is expected. He anticipated his monthly salary means he went out and spent it before he received it. But nowadays usage is looser. He anticipated inclement weather means he took an umbrella. But it's a distinction only pedants draw.

Embarrassed has two of everything in it (2 x e, a, r, s). **Harassed** has only 1 x r. I would be embarrassed if I spelt harassed like embarrassed.

Similarly **accommodation** has 2 x a, c, m and 3 x o.

Practice is the noun (practice makes perfect) whereas **practise** is the verb (you must practise every day). Similarly with **licence** (noun) and **license** (verb).

Affect is the verb and **effect** the noun. An effect is the result of something being affected. Effect is only used as a verb in one strict sense and that is to effect a change.

Fewer of things that can be counted, **less** of volume. He used less mortar but laid fewer bricks. If more people knew this there would be fewer mistakes. If fewer people know it there will be more mistakes. (People goes with fewer since people can be counted.)

A **principal** is a top or sole person (the principal of a school is the head teacher). A **principle** is a point of belief or conviction (it ends in 'le' like 'rule'). The principal was a principled person means the head teacher was someone who had an ethical code.

The abbreviation **e.g.** means 'for example' in Latin. But it's increasingly confused with **i.e.** (which means 'that is' from the Latin 'id est'). The forest was made up of trees (i.e. oaks) means the forest was made up only of oak trees. The forest was made up of trees (e.g. oaks) means the forest was made up of trees including some oaks.

With **numbers** whether you use words or figures is generally a matter of house style. Many organisations use words for one to nine then from 10 on they use figures (not a rule I've particularly followed in this book).

Different should be followed by **from** (this is different from that) except in American when 'than' is used (this is different than that). But **compared** is followed by **with**. It is tempting (but wrong) to say 'different to' and 'compared to'.

All right and **always**. Never 'alright'. Never 'allways'.

Between where two are involved. **Among** where there are several.

Unique means one of a kind which is why nothing can be 'very unique'.

Criteria is the plural of criterion, so you cannot say: 'The selection criteria is…' but only 'are'. **Data** too is plural so it's correct to say: 'The data are'.

Who is the doer and **whom** the done to. Who did this? To whom am I speaking?

Myself is best avoided. 'If you need assistance, please contact Henry or myself' is wrong. It should be '…Henry or me'. There are only two good uses. The first is if 'myself' is the object of the verb and the subject and object are the same, so for example: to control oneself; to lose oneself; to know oneself. The second is for emphasis: I did it myself; I ate all the cake myself (i.e. I didn't share it).

Often people use 'myself' because they think 'me' isn't business-like. Or they don't know when to use **me** or **I**. The tip here is to drop the other person from the sentence: 'Henry and me went to the meeting' is wrong because when you drop out Henry you are left with 'Me went to the meeting'. It is: 'I went to the meeting' which is why it's also: 'Henry and I went to the meeting'.

Take the earlier example: 'Please contact Henry or myself'. Drop Henry and it becomes 'Please contact myself' which is clearly wrong – you wouldn't even say it. What you'd say is: 'Please contact me.' So too: 'Please contact Henry or me.'

Hopefully is a useless word. If people use it to mean 'I hope' they should say that instead. I hope they won't use hopefully from now on.

So too with **literally**. It means 'to the word'. A literal translation means a translation that is word for word regardless of sense (which means that it may be unintelligible). However, it came to mean 'actually' as in 'he was literally speechless with anger' meaning that he was so angry he actually could not speak. More recently it has come to be a way of adding emphasis regardless of actuality (I was literally over the moon with joy). Best to avoid it especially when writing.

While we're on pet hates, don't tell me something is **very important**. Very seems to have the opposite from its intended effect. Very important sounds less than important. It risks sounding hysterical. And ration the number of times you use **important** itself. Of course it's important. Why would you be wasting your time writing and mine reading if it wasn't?

Be **consistent** in your use of the singular or plural. A firm of accountants can be it (the firm) or they (accountants). Choose one and stick with it. If in doubt use the singular with words like firm, company, department, team, group and organisation unless you are referring specifically to the people in them. There is a tendency now to use the plural if the immediately preceding noun is plural too. 'A crowd of crows' should be singular (a crowd 'is') but the tendency (incorrect though it is) is to say: 'A crowd of crows are' because the noun immediately preceding the verb (crows) is plural.

Try not to **split infinitives**. An infinitive is a verb with the word 'to' in front of it. 'To go' is an infinitive. In *Star Trek* the catchphrase 'to boldly go' splits the infinitive by inserting an adverb between 'to' and 'go'. This is considered poor practice but only because in Latin you couldn't do it (the infinitive of a verb was always a single word so could not be split). My view is: avoid it if possible; do it if absolutely necessary for emphasis or the cadence (rhythm) of a sentence.

Punctuation

Words are one thing. You can look them up. People are more freaked by punctuation, both in how to use it and in being offended when they see a usage with which they disagree.

Punctuation is the set of symbols that separate words on a page. It has only one purpose: to help readers navigate their way through your text. Its usage changes over time which is why people regularly have bust-ups over the correct use of commas.

I follow some simple rules that are designed not to cause offence to pedants. Let's start with apostrophes.

Apostrophes

Most people reveal their lack of confidence about language in their use of apostrophes. An apostrophe often represents one or more missing letters – usually because there's been a contraction: two words have been stuck together and as a result one or more letters left out.

So, for example, **it's** is short for **it is** and **he's** is short for **he is**.

The confusion comes with possessives (meaning 'of' or 'for'). The basic rule is that possessive pronouns do not have apostrophes. He is the pronoun. Belonging to him is **his**. She is the pronoun. Belonging to her is **hers**. It is the pronoun. Belonging to it is **its**. They is the pronoun. Belonging to them is **theirs**. Similarly with us and **ours** and you and **yours** (hence 'Yours Is No Disgrace' by classic prog rock band Yes). No apostrophes in any of that lot.

For everything else you need an apostrophe. The problem is usually where to put it. In general you can follow your ear. If you want to say 'the book belonging to Amanda' you would say 'Amanda's book' and you would know where to put the apostrophe because you wouldn't say 'Amanda book'. You'd add an 's' and the apostrophe would obviously go before the 's': 'Amanda's book'.

You do this even if the person to whom the book belongs ends in 's'. So 'the book belonging to Chris' becomes 'Chris's book'. This is generally what people say so again you can be guided by your ear.

The confusion arises with plurals which end in an 's'. In this case you just add an apostrophe. (Plurals which don't end in an 's' aren't a problem: the book of the children becomes 'the children's book'.)

Take the following:

> Partners meeting

There is obviously an apostrophe missing, but where to put it?

The tip here is to deconstruct the phrase to get back to what it would otherwise have been. If it's the meeting of or for the partner (in the singular) then write that down like this:

> Partner meeting

In other words it's a meeting of one partner, in the singular. So add an 's' and the apostrophe in the usual way:

> Partner's meeting

But if actually when you deconstruct it you come out with this: meeting of or for the partners (in the plural) you write that down like this:

> Partners meeting

This is a plural ending in an 's' so you simply add an apostrophe:

> Partners' meeting

While we're on apostrophes, **Dos and Don'ts** is correct. Do's and Don't's isn't. And (although I admit this is a matter of preference rather than rule) for the same reason I write 1970s not 1970's.

Consistently inconsistent

The eagle-eyed will have spotted that I have been inconsistent in my use of inverted commas throughout this book. Sometimes I've been using inverted commas, for instance when saying 's', and at other times I haven't, for instance just now when writing 1970s. The reason for this is to avoid confusing you when talking about the use of apostrophes, since the two look the same and, at other times, when too many would look messy. I defend a departure from a rule of grammar or from consistency when the purpose is to make the reader's life easier.

Commas

Commas give people almost as much trouble as apostrophes. But they are simpler. For punctuation use stops where possible. If you have to use commas, use them either singly or in pairs.

Never use a comma to join two sentences. So do not write: 'We have received your request, however we are unable to agree to it.' This should be two sentences: 'We have received your request. However, we....'

(Originally you were never supposed to use 'however' at the start of a sentence. It had to follow the verb: 'We are unable, however, to agree to it'. Nowadays you can start a sentence with 'however' but put a comma after it.)

Commas used singly act as a breathing point for the reader (remember not throttling the reader?). Generally you are not supposed to use a comma before 'and'. To do so is American usage (in the States they call it the Oxford comma and blame the Brits). My view is that it is fine to do so as a breathing point (which is what commas are used in America to do).

Commas are also used as separators. So you generally use a comma between two adjectives – the big, black cat. But you know what I think about adjectives.

But the most versatile use of commas is in pairs where they work like brackets. They bracket off a sub-clause in a sentence. The test is: does the sentence still read properly if the text between the brackets is deleted? He went inside, thinking it was about to rain, and found his umbrella. This works because, with the text between commas omitted, the sentence still reads grammatically (just as this one does). He went inside and found his umbrella.

Don't put a comma after a bracket, unless you think the bracketed section makes the sentence so long that the reader needs a pause. Even then the second bracket usually acts as a pause anyway.

Brackets (also known as parentheses)

Using brackets is one way of getting round the need to write short sentences (by putting a sub-clause between parentheses, like this). But be careful. Brackets make a sentence look complex, dense and off-putting. They can also sound too cautious (every assertion is followed by a bracketed caveat) and just downright irritating when they sound like a succession of asides interrupting a conversation.

I was prone to overuse of brackets when I started out as a journalist. I cured myself by using dashes instead – like this – because they look more dynamic and flowing.

The issue over where to put the full stop when using brackets is easy. Where the bracket opens within a sentence, it should close before the full stop (like this). (But where the bracketed language is a sentence and the initial bracket precedes the start of the sentence, the second one should fall after the full stop, like this.)

Quotation marks

Whether quotation marks should fall inside or outside stops follows a similar rule. If you are quoting a full sentence it begins and ends within quotation marks.

> 'Generally, quote marks go around the outside of the other punctuation marks,' he said.

> He said, 'You preface a quote mark with a comma or a colon and you start the speech with a capital letter.'

The problem comes when 'only part of a sentence is reported speech'. Then the end-quote mark can fall before the full stop.

Here I've used both 'quotation' and 'quote'. The first is correct, the second colloquial. Just as 'invitation' is correct and 'invite' colloquial (which is why people criticise 'invite').

Semi-colons (;) and colons (:)

The most common use for semi-colons is in a list after a colon (mentioned in the chapter on layout).

A list starts with a colon followed by:

- each item on a new line;
- a lower case letter at the start of each line;
- a semi-colon at the end of each line;
- the last but one item (the penultimate item) ending with a semi-colon followed by the word 'and'; and
- a full-stop at the end of the final item.

This is called a bulleted list (each dot at the start of a line is a bullet).

It could be written as a narrative list. A narrative list starts with a colon followed by: each item following on the same line; a lower case letter at the start of each item; a semi-colon separating each item; until the final item which starts with 'and'; and which ends with a full-stop.

You can see now why in business bulleted lists are preferred to narrative lists. They are visual and easier to read.

There is a more informal version of the bulleted list which is this:

- Start each item with a capital letter
- Omit semi-colons at the end of each line
- Omit 'and' at the end of the penultimate line
- Do without a stop at the end of the final item

You'll see that each line starts with a capital letter and there is no punctuation at the end. This is what Word does automatically. Some people put a final full stop after the final item. But I think it looks cleaner without. It shows you are disregarding punctuation completely rather than attempting to do what is traditional but getting it wrong (as some critical readers might think). Lawyers sometimes insert that penultimate 'and' just to make sure readers know you need all the items and that the list isn't a set of alternatives of which you just need one.

The more traditional use of semi-colons is to separate two complete sentences linked by topic or theme. So for example:

> Semi-colons look antiquated; they are best avoided.

Colons are used at the beginning of a list but they can also be used where an explanation follows an assertion or statement. So:

> He was angry: he'd missed the train.

My preference is to keep it simple and just use stops.

> Semi-colons look antiquated. They are best avoided.

> He was angry. He'd missed the train.

'And' and 'But' at starts of sentences

My writing style depends a lot on starting sentences with 'and' or 'but'. 'And' is more controversial than 'but', although increasingly accepted. Don't do it if you can avoid it. And only do it if you know the reader won't mind. And don't do it with successive sentences. It becomes tedious and juvenile. (A good argument to keep in your back pocket if challenged is that William Blake started what is known as *Jerusalem* with 'And did those feet…'.)

The way to avoid issues with punctuation is by keeping it simple. Keeping it simple is where we're headed next.

CHAPTER 9

KEEPING IT SIMPLE

Poor writing is a failure of thought – each statement should be a bridge that flows to the next – editing is mainly about moving sections around so the ideas are in the right order – identifying the core and stripping away whatever's not relevant – the real experts can explain things simply – asking simple questions – simple is best – this is what clients love – commercial leases – windows – service charge cap – smiley faces – CIMA article – Dear Bill: you were right – professional liability – why clients use us – technical expertise, experience and judgement – simplicity in business – strategy – slogans – simple is hard to achieve – being persuasive – making it personal – building a connection – developing your voice – breaking the rules – Orwell – Hemingway's *Death In The Afternoon* – jukeboxes

The last chapter is where you might have expected me to start the whole book. After all, problems with writing are problems with language, aren't they?

But as you will have gathered, poor writing is not really a failure of language, or merely a failure of language.

It's a failure of other things too – in fact, principally of other things: failure to Think Reader; failure to get to the point; failure to revise the first draft; and so on.

Failure of thought

Poor writing is not usually the result of poor language. It's usually the result of poor logic. If you set out what you want to say in a logical manner where each statement is a bridge that flows from the previous one and leads to the next the reader will be taken seamlessly along like a train on a track. The reader won't be able to get off or deviate or stop. In fact the reader won't want to.

As an editor I found most of my work focused on moving sections of articles around so the ideas were in the right order and made a more compelling flow. I wasn't changing the words my writers and contributors used. I was changing the order of their paragraphs. Much less was about correcting individual uses of language. I saw my job as simplifying: identifying the core of the piece and putting it up front; then stripping away anything that wasn't strictly relevant.

It is still my core skill: knowing the order in which to put things; rather than knowing the right or best words to use. If you get the order right the rest follows. It's one thing to edit what is already there. I have never found that especially difficult. But to write like this in the first place is not easy. To keep things simple you have to leave a lot out. The challenge lies in knowing what.

Simple is clever

As a legal and financial journalist I often interviewed bankers and lawyers to understand the latest financial instruments and transactions. By training I was a banking lawyer myself so this was stuff I should have been able to understand. But some of these innovations were so cutting edge they took a lot of explaining.

Often I would spend up to two hours with one of these market professionals (I would be writing about them and their organisations which was great publicity for them, so they were happy to spend the time helping me get it right). On a number of occasions I would emerge from these meetings with my head pounding, totally confused. Originally I thought it was me. I was the idiot.

Then gradually I realised two things.

First, the really clever people who understand something completely can explain it in very simple terms, however complex it really is. These people were riveting. They were exciting to talk to. They made you understand. They didn't talk down to you or patronise you. They brought you into the complexity of their world but did so by making it seem easy.

Second, the simple question is always the best. I would find myself in a press conference in a hall with a load of other journalists and some bigwig droning on at a podium at the front and if I didn't understand my hand would go up and I would ask the bigwig to explain it again more simply. And lo and behold, all these other hacks who'd been scribbling away, making copious notes (I hadn't because how can you write something down if you don't understand it?) would look up and nod in agreement. They weren't getting it too. So I had done us all a favour.

These things taught me that simple is best. But you need a lot of guts to be simple. There is nowhere to hide when you are using simple language and addressing the client as you. You have to be clear as water. Anything less than that will be obviously fudged.

What clients want

Most professionals lack this degree of self-confidence, however good they are. But in my experience it is what clients love. They love the expert who can make things simple. Heaven knows, the rest of their lives are complex enough. If you can get an adviser who is clear all the time about the ins and outs of what you are trying to do they are worth their weight in gold. Clients don't pay us for long documents. They pay us for expertise that genuinely helps them and adds value.

Two examples – both about commercial property – spring to mind. One day at a law firm where I worked I was passing the office of the head of real estate. He had a monstrously large document on his desk and he was poring over it line by line. This was a City law firm and we were used to big documents but this was horrific. It was a Moby Dick of a legal tome. I asked him what it was. It was the lease for a floor of a recently built City skyscraper. We were advising a large firm of accountants who were about to move in.

'My goodness, Donald, that looks awful,' I said.

He shook his head. 'Not really. There's only one issue.'

'What's that?'

'Windows. Who's responsible for the windows?'

What he meant was that the rest of it was reasonably standard, as commercial leases often are. But in a skyscraper a big bit of expenditure is maintenance of windows (just getting access can take a crane) and of course liability and insurance cover if a massive pane of glass falls off the building and into the street below.

This particular partner was vastly experienced. Clients loved the fact that he cut through the inconsequential stuff and got to the big issues. But that takes guts. It takes guts to say that we won't waste time and money arguing over the other stuff.

The other example is more of the same (also commercial property; also a lease – I chose it for that reason) but it affected me personally. At a different time in my life I ran a small business. The business took a lease of the top floor of an attractive period building in the centre of a well-to-do town. Although I was a lawyer I didn't make the mistake of doing the legal stuff myself. I passed the lease to a property lawyer I knew called Tim. I didn't want this done as a favour. As I told Tim, I wanted to be able to sue him if it went wrong (some client and friend I was!). He looked through it and said: 'There's plenty I could go back to them about' – the landlord was a major insurance company, so it was a typically thorough and onerous set of terms – 'but the only big issue is the service charge. I'm going to cap it at £2,500 a year.' He did and the landlord agreed.

It was an old building and under standard commercial repairing covenants the tenant is liable for almost all the expenditure the landlord incurs on a building. Basically the tenant pays for the building's upgrade. And that's what happened. Three years later the owner of the highly successful recruitment agency downstairs passed me in the corridor. 'Have you seen the service charge this year?' he said. I admitted I hadn't because mine was capped so that's what I paid year-in, year-out. Now his premises were at least twice the size of mine. But his bill for the service charge for that year had been a massive £40,000. Tim had saved me from almost certain penury.

What has this got to do with writing? Nothing. What has it got to do with giving clients what they want? Everything. And this is what our writing must also achieve for clients.

Smiley faces

A colleague of mine who's a pensions lawyer had to provide complex advice to the trustees of the pension fund of a big company, a household name. He put up a slide showing the six pages of advice he had prepared. 'That's what I've prepared for you,' he said. 'But this is actually what you want.' And he put up a slide of a single smiley face. 'You just want to know that what you're proposing to do is OK.' Of course, he couldn't say yes. That's because the regulations were so complex, both to understand and apply.

So what he had done was to take these enormously complex regulations and reduce them to a series of flowcharts that took into account all possibilities and variations. If Yes go up here. If No go down there. And so on. It took a long time for him to do and was therefore expensive in terms of fees. But the trustees loved it. They could use it immediately and it was simple enough for their entire team to apply. Now that's not even words. In fact what amazes me in this story is that lawyers who, after all, are wordy people, can grasp so profoundly the importance of pictures.

I have in a file a cutting from a 1996 issue of CIMA's magazine. CIMA is the Chartered Institute of Management Accountants – basically management accountants work in, and are employed by, companies. I tore this article out and have kept it ever since because it said the best way of conveying financial information to non-financial people is by using smiley faces. It developed this idea into quite a complex set of symbols – size of nose for cash flow, angle of eyebrows for profit, and so on. That degree of complexity, I thought, was missing the point a bit. Straightforward smiling or frowning faces were good because they were simple. But I was still impressed with the overall emphasis on visual impact and the simplicity of using a face. Many businesses use traffic lights: green OK, amber warning, red bad. It's the same idea.

I was wrong

The best letter of advice from a lawyer to a client I have ever seen was one line long. It said: 'Bill – you were right and I was wrong.' That is a very ballsy statement. Implicit in it are lots of things.

First, that the lawyer and client were having an intense and detailed discussion. That must mean it was about the law, so the client was also probably a lawyer or an equal professional (accountant, tax expert) who knew the law in this area.

Two, they had the ideal professional / client relationship where you can say exactly what you think.

Three, the client would not use this letter to sue the lawyer – and the lawyer knew it. This means they had a very close professional relationship built on mutual respect and trust.

Four, the client was a busy man who didn't like procrastinating nonsense. Obviously what had happened was that in a meeting the lawyer had given a preliminary view but had said he would need to look it up to see which of their interpretations was the right one. In this instance the client's was. But you can tell from the brevity of the letter that this admission was in no way going to damage their relationship. Indeed its brevity would serve only to strengthen the relationship. The client knew the lawyer was good. He wasn't going to stop using him just because of this. In fact he'd use him more. If you have an adviser who comes clean on everything you can trust them with your life.

All of these points we can glean from just eight words.

Professional liability

Professionals tell me all the time you can't be like this because you'll be sued. I don't agree. First, why would a client sue an adviser with whom they have such a personal understanding? Second, just because you're wrong it doesn't mean you're negligent. I have worked in some of the best and largest law firms in the world, either as an employee or a consultant. These people do cutting edge work where the law is unclear and the commercial circumstances are completely novel. In this sort of area you are in space: it's never been done before. You can get the best, most experienced brains in the world and it still may not work. They have not been negligent. They have not been lacking in due care. At this level it's a matter of finely calibrated judgement. This is what clients pay advisers for. And at this level they are prepared to pay a lot and still feel it's value for money.

Besides, I certainly don't believe that the way to reduce the risk of being sued is by using impenetrable language so the client can't justifiably rely on your advice. Why else are they using you and are you charging them the sort of fees that expert professionals can command?

When you are working at this rarefied a level, in the stratosphere of big business, and you are using simple language to explain things briefly and clearly, you are a star.

So you need to tell clients what they need to know. And if you don't know or the answer isn't clear, tell them it isn't and why it isn't. Don't just use unclear language. In other words I'd much prefer, as a client, to receive something that says: 'Chris – the position isn't clear. This is because [reason]. However, my view is [whatever it is]. I may be wrong because [reason]. But I've come across similar positions in the past where [this happened]. So although I can't be completely sure, I think the best route would be [whatever it is].'

Why clients use us

That, to me, is helpful advice, based on technical expertise, experience and judgement – the three reasons why clients use professional advisers.

Technical expertise is knowledge of our discipline. Experience is knowing how that expertise applies in practice to real-life situations. Judgement is a sense of the right thing to do in any set of circumstances (whether or not they've been encountered before). And it's this last that clients are really paying us for and judge us by.

Technical expertise they take for granted (and often can't tell if we have or not, but assume we do – they judge us on our use of language as a proxy).

Experience comes from having done (something like) it before. Judgement is partly a reflection of the other two (having deep technical knowledge and experience of how it applies in practice) but is also innate. It is what makes a great professional. This is why the greatest professionals use the simplest language. They know their subject so well, they have nothing to hide. Indeed they spend their lives educating clients and colleagues in it. And for that you need simple language.

Simplicity in business

There is a parallel here with business in general. Apart from being involved in writing and editing, much of my working life has been about helping professionals with business development and strategy. And to my mind the simplest strategies are the best.

Business is complex, no question (and by business I mean government too – the business of government). But brilliant business leaders make it simple. They state their goals simply. The implementation of those goals will be complex and demanding but if the vision is clear and succinct so that everyone can share it and get behind it, the plan is likely to be successful.

In fact I'd go so far as to say that, unless you can express a business strategy clearly (for instance, explain what makes the business different, known as the unique selling proposition) in a single sentence or at the most two, it is unlikely to succeed. There's a reason why Hollywood producers want to know what the story idea is in a single sentence (shark terrorises beach – *Jaws*; hobbit fights himself and others to rid the world of evil ring – etc, etc).

Take these examples of business strategies:

To put a man on the moon

(NASA in the 1960s)

To put a refrigerator in every American home

(General Electric after World War II)

To put a computer on every desk

(Microsoft when computers were massive mainframes)

All of these successful strategies had one thing in common. They were all simple. Anyone involved could understand the vision and do their bit to make it happen.

That's why simple language appeals to the best leaders. They understand its importance.

Think of the following trademarked marketing slogans.

Just do it (Nike).

Because I'm worth it (L'Oréal).

Does what it says on the tin (Ronseal).

How hard can simple be – in business?

But don't make the mistake of thinking that simple is simple to do. How many expensive copywriters in advertising agencies did it take to come up with that lot? Quite a few, I would hazard.

Steve Jobs was a self-driven genius. He made life for those around him difficult and he probably wasn't the happiest of men, never really at peace with himself. But his mantra was simplicity. He used to spend more time in Jon Ives's design laboratory on the Apple campus tinkering with shapes and materials and how things felt and worked than anywhere else except his modest study at home, empty as a monk's cell, which passers-by on the pavement could look through the window into (Jobs didn't live in a swanky gated mansion – his house backed on to the street).

All the time he would shout at staff: simple, make it simple. I've never heard anyone say he was an idiot. That's why people liked working for him and found him inspiring. He gave their work purpose.

Jobs described the iPod when it first came out as *a thousand tunes in your pocket*. Simple. Memorable. I suspect he made that up himself.

How hard can simple be – in writing?

Hemingway still seems contemporary because his language, being simple, is timeless. It will not go out of date.

Hemingway's first best seller was *A Farewell To Arms*. The final paragraph is just three sentences long. It has fewer than 50 words. Yet Hemingway rewrote that final paragraph 47 times. In the final version three quarters of the words are monosyllables.

Cézanne painted pictures that you can get immediately. They look simple to produce. But they took years and thousands of minute applications of the correct colour to achieve their dazzling but simple effects. Simple isn't easy but it's what our clients pay us for. As Dolly Parton said: It costs a lot to look this cheap.

Being persuasive

People ask me how they can write persuasively. You can only persuade by deploying arguments that convince – that are rational and logical. But you need readers to read what those arguments are. To do that you need to do everything I've suggested so far. But there is something more. Persuasive writing is about persuading readers to read what you have written – and to keep reading. I think this is about engaging them.

When I ask people to nominate a piece of writing or a writer they like and then ask them the reason for their choice it usually comes down to a sense of connection.

Making it personal

One way of doing this is to make it personal. If the reader feels you are speaking to them they are more likely to continue listening (reading). They will feel you are reaching out to them as a person (warm) and this is more compelling than an impersonal, objective style (cold). Being personal starts to establish a rapport with the reader that makes it harder for him or her to turn away (it's easier to stop reading than turn your back on someone speaking to you). The authorial voice is speaking to you. It's apparently why people like my books. I don't see them as writing but as talking. To you. Being personal means being human – and people are more interested in each other than in things.

Of course this does not suit every reader. And what the reader wants matters most. But most readers will forgive your style if it is compelling.

It's why I suggested that you read out what you have written. If you can't imagine yourself saying something aloud, then you probably shouldn't write it. It doesn't necessarily follow that you should write the way you speak. Like, you may not, like, speak, like articulately. But, if you do, fine.

This is what allows you (within reason) to break the rules, to use language that is all right when spoken but might raise eyebrows when written down. But this isn't everybody's cup of tea (a more formal way of saying that is: not to everyone's taste; but I like cup of tea – it's more colloquial).

Being appropriate

I admit it isn't always appropriate. There are times when writing has to be institutional. Formal writing requires a more objective, impersonal approach. *It appears* rather than *I think*. There are times when formality is desirable: the minutes of the parish council; an announcement from Buckingham Palace; a court order. Similarly in a business context: a company's annual results; an announcement to shareholders; the CEO's state-of-the-union to employees.

What matters – as always – is what the reader expects in the specific context. You have to balance up what keeps the reader's interest and makes for a faster read against what the reader might find offensive or might damage your credibility in the reader's eyes.

Being personal leads to another way in which you will over time become persuasive, in the sense that your professional credibility will increase so that clients come to trust you and do as you suggest. This is through developing your own style. It must still do what I've talked about at length in this book. But it must also be you. And this is where you can start to break the rules I've set out because you won't need them any more. You will have become a consummate professional. You will be talking to your clients all the time. You will know what they want. You will have developed a personal style of communication that suits both them and you. In short your voice will be heard in your writing.

Developing your voice and breaking the rules

If in your writing you can develop your voice, readers will read to the end and they will come back for more. The way you write will be an integral part of the advice you give and the job that you do. By then it will have nothing to do with what's set out in this book.

In other words the rules and strictures I have set out here are only to get you started in the right direction. They will enable you to do what you must in your role to be a credible professional, credible to bosses and clients alike. But as you gain in experience and confidence you will find your own way, your own style. And then this book will have served its purpose.

George Orwell's final rule about good writing is to break any rule of grammar rather than write something downright barbarous (or words to that effect). I like this. It essentially means: do whatever is necessary to help the reader even if it means flouting convention.

I've been referring to Hemingway throughout as the master of brevity. The final chapter of his book *Death In The Afternoon* starts with a statement that if he had made it enough of a book it would have had everything about Spain in it. Then he puts a colon. Then Hemingway lists, separated by semi-colons, everything about Spain that he loved. Result: a single sentence that runs to several pages. It must be one of the longest – and most brilliant – sentences in the English language.

Writing is an extension of our personalities – which is why we take any criticism personally. But you can turn the personal to your advantage. In my case I am also a poet. This doesn't have a direct bearing on what I am doing here but my editor has spotted an awareness of rhythm even in my emails at work – which again helps to make my writing at work a better read. (That Ted Hughes line I quoted earlier is in fact an iambic pentameter. But do you know what? Who cares!)

Being professional about our writing, as we are in every other facet of our working lives, means rising above the personal. I once wrote a piece about jukeboxes (I had one at the time) for a national newspaper. When the piece came out there were only three words I recognised from the draft I'd submitted: 'Christopher', 'Stoakes' and 'jukebox'. The paper still paid me.

CHAPTER 10

~~CONCLUSION~~

Write it, rewrite it, then write it again – sometimes the obvious isn't right –
writing training that didn't involve writing – value for money – less is more
– being self-critical – gas kills – stay humble – writing is just a medium for
conveying ideas – it should be invisible – writing is just part of the job

Since I've been saying all along that readers don't read to the end I'm not expecting you to be reading this.

But if you are, I feel I owe you an apology. This book is about getting to the point, putting the most important thing up front and being succinct. Yet it has taken me this long to set it all out. So you may have got every impression that I wrote this book to find out what I wanted to say about writing and then didn't go back and rewrite it once I knew. In other words I haven't done what I've been screaming at you all along to do.

But in actual fact that's not so.

What I actually did was write it, then go back and rewrite it. Doing that reduced the original to a few pages of rules and principles. I got right to the point. I made it as succinct as possible. And you do know what? It was unreadable. It was so boring and obvious. Even my editor said so.

So I had to go back and write it for the third time and put everything back in. Because although you are my client (having bought this book) and my reader, this is not like a professional relationship where the client just wants the answer and isn't fundamentally interested in how we got there.

Here you need to have been with me every step of the way if you are to know why I think these things and why, therefore, you should consider doing them yourself. As I say, none of this is difficult. When reduced to a half-dozen tips and techniques it's all pretty obvious. But sometimes the obvious doesn't turn out to be right after all.

I was once asked by a practice of professional advisers to devise some writing training for them. The first thing I said was: 'If this is just another Dos & Don'ts it will die a death. It will be too boring.'

A YouTube about writing?

In the end my editor and I (we work on these things together too) came up with an idea which is still the best bit of training design I've been involved in (and that includes others which have won awards). We asked each of four professionals, regarded within the practice as among the best at writing, to choose a piece they were proudest of.

We then filmed each one answering some standard questions about their particular piece. Who was the client? What was the issue? What did they know about the client's preferences when it came to written advice? What structure did they adopt and why? How hard was it to write? And so on. And we edited these interviews down to no more than ten minutes each.

We put them on the firm's intranet together with a PDF of the advice itself so that someone watching the interview at his or her monitor could access the piece itself while listening to the author of the piece discuss it. We did the thing entirely in-house and our little training programme proved a huge success across the practice.

It was training about writing but those being trained watched and listened and didn't write a single word while the interviewees simply talked. In other words, to get across key messages about writing we didn't do the conventional thing of getting participants to write.

So with this book. I started to weave in my own views on writing and how I had learnt. I included some stories. And the book took off. I'm not saying it's perfect. But it's a lot better than it would have been. I think I understood intuitively that readers wouldn't want a rule book. They would want context and explanation. And since I have a background in business development it made sense to couch this discussion in the context of professionals advising clients. I think I was feeling my way to what readers would want. I may not have succeeded. But I think I realised this book needed to be a little bit for entertainment and not just for action.

That's why this book isn't as short as it might have been.

Value for money?

But in case you're thinking it's too short for the cover price, I still ended up with a draft that was twice this length.

So you're paying for the time I took to cut it back down.

You say you would have preferred to pay less and got more?

You wouldn't, you know. Trust me. You would have read even less of that than you have of this. So the cost per page would have been the same.

I am being self-critical for a reason. I said in the last chapter that good writing is the result of good thinking, not (just) good language. It is also the result of a mindset. You need to remain self-critical.

The laugh was on me

I was running a day-long programme on writing in the workplace. It was an open programme. Anyone could book to come on it. One of the exercises I set (more to give the participants a break from my voice than anything else) was to edit down a piece. The piece was this:

> It is important to keep at the forefront of your mind that carbon monoxide is very dangerous. It is absolutely critical that you take every possible and conceivable precaution. In particular, this deadly and potentially fatal gas can become highly concentrated in very enclosed places, resulting in extremely dangerous levels of toxicity usually leading to lethal consequences. In view of the above, it follows that it is up to you to take all necessary precautions and failure to do so will be your sole responsibility.

It's not a great exercise, I'll grant you. But that's not the point. All day long a fellow at the back had been staring out of the window. He had been getting on my nerves. During the exercise he continued to stare out of the window. After a few minutes I asked the room (about thirty people in all) how many words they had managed to reduce it to.

I started at 20 words or fewer (about a third of the room stuck their hands up) then brought it down to 10 or under (just a handful left). Finally there were just two at 5 words or under (one on 4, the other on 3). The bloke at the back was still staring out of the window. So I decided to pick on him.

'Would you mind sharing with the rest of us how many words you managed to reduce it to?'

'Two.'

'Really?' I was genuinely interested. If so, he was the winner. 'What were they?'

'Gas kills.'

That served me right. Stay humble. There's always a faster gun in the west.

In the end it doesn't matter

The purpose of good writing is to keep out of the reader's way. Writing is just a medium for conveying ideas. It should be invisible.

This, I think is the ideal mindset, that writing is a job or part of a job – one that we all think we do well but we don't.

I hope this book has been helpful. Please tell me what you think so I can improve it. I hope you may even have kept reading to the end (or, more likely, just turned to this page to see how it panned out).

Either way, if you have, it's not because I'm a good writer but because I've got a great editor, who is always my first reader.

VJ, this one's for you.

I hope it's the one you wanted.

INDEX

A

A Farewell To Arms 76
A Life Of Privilege, Mostly..................25
Action...1, 2
Active(s) 29, 31, 32
Acts of Parliament.............................15
Adjectives 29, 32
Adverbs...29, 32
American spellings.............................60
Anglicised (English) spelling..............60
Anglo-Saxon 29, 30
Antithesis 4
Apostrophes...........................59, 60, 63
Apple...76
Argument(s) 1, 4
Attachments...............................51, 57
Authorial voice 77

B

Bar chart 48
Bibliographies 7, 9, 10
Blake, Wiliam......................................67
Botsford, Gardner 25
Boxed copy...48
Boxes...45, 49
Brackets...59, 65
Branding 35
Bulleted list(s) 45, 59
Bullets..48

C

Carbon copy 2
Cézanne 76
Churchill, Winston..............................31
Circadian rhythms..................17, 20, 49
Clichés..32
Client(s) ...2, 3, 4, 5, 10, 12, 13, 15, 23, 24
Colloquial..77
Colons...59, 66
Continuous loop, the...........................7
Customer is king, the......................1, 2

Commas 65
Complex constructions 14
Conclusion......................1, 7, 9, 37, 41
Connecting phrases 41
Continuous improvement 7
Continuous internal loop.....................8
Copy 49
Copy editors 33
Counter-argument(s) 1, 4
Covey, Stephen...........................17, 26
Criticism..............17, 21, 23, 24, 78, 81
Cross-heads 46, 47
Customer(s) 2, 4, 10, 12, 13

D

Death In The Afternoon 78
Denning, Lord....................................45
Developing your voice 69
Double negatives...............................44

E

Economist, The 39, 42
Editing 15, 20, 42
Editor 12, 17, 19, 21, 22, 23, 24, 25, 31, 42, 49, 55, 70, 78, 82, 84
Email(s) ..35, 50, 51, 52, 53, 54, 55, 56, 57
Emboldening 45, 47
Entertainment 1, 2, 8
Err on the side of caution 10, 11, 57
Essay(s) 1, 4, 5
Exclamation marks 47
Executive summary 34, 39, 44, 49
External clients 3

F

Facebook...vii
Facts..43
FAQs (Frequently Asked Questions) 45, 48
Fiction..18
First draft 17, 18, 19, 20

Flow diagram 48
Fonts..35
Footnotes........................7, 9, 10, 45
Formal writing 77
Format 57
Funny emails 51
G
General electric..............................75
Get to the point ....viii, 25
Getting your point across................. vii
Good Prose...................................19
Grammar...........................22, 59, 60
H
Hard copy 49
Heading(s) 35, 46, 49
Headline(s) 33, 34, 35, 36, 42, 56
Hemingway, Ernest....17, 18, 26, 76, 78
Hopefully.......................................62
House style....29, 35, 45, 46, 47, 49, 61
How to stop....................................37
Hughes, Ted 30, 79
I
Iambic pentameter...........................79
Image..35
Impersonal.....................................77
Information..............................1, 2, 5
Internal clients.................................3
Internet..8
Introduction...............................1, 7, 9
Inverted commas 60
J
Jargon......................................14, 15
Jerusalem 67
Jobs, Steve....................................76
Joyce, James.............................17, 19
K
Kidder, Tracy 19
King, Stephen 2, 17, 18, 20
L
L'Oréal 76
Language..........................7, 14, 15, 22

Larkin, Philip...............................7, 12
Latin..15, 61
Latin roots..................................29, 30
Letter(s) 2, 51, 53
Leonard, Elmore..............................24
Literature 18
Long sentences 14
Long words.....................................14
Look of the page..............................47
Lord Of The Rings 57
M
Make it personal 77
Marketing, definition 4
Maverick 34
Means to an end..............................24
Meeting clients' needs profitably 4
Memo(s) ......vii, 2, 5, 34, 35, 53, 56, 60
Methodology 5
Microsoft..75
Monosyllable(s) 29, 30
N
NASA..75
Negative(s) 32
Neuro-Linguistic Programming..........55
Nike 76
Nominalisation 33
Nouns 33
Numbered paragraphs 45, 47
O
Object 31
On Writing 18
One side long 29, 34
Opening paragraph 7, 41
Orwell, George 14, 30, 32, 69, 78
P
Paragraph(s) 19, 33, 47, 70
Parentheses 59, 65
Parton, Dolly...................................76
Passive(s)...........................29, 31, 32
Personal 77
Phone 53

Phone call 51, 52, 55

Phonetic 60

Pie chart 48

Plural subjects 37

Politics And The English Language ...30

Pompous language 14

Poor thinking viii

Poor writing viii

Positive(s) 32

PowerPoint 48

Presentation(s) .... vi, 48

Professional writer vii

Prose 18

Punctuation 59, 63

Puns 33

Purple passage(s) 17, 24

Purpose of writing at work 1, 2

Putting the reader first 7, 11

Pyramid 29

Q

Quotation marks 59, 66

R

Reader 24, 70

Reader comes first 1, 2

Reader wants to stop reading 7, 8

Re-imagining 25

Reluctant reader 1

Repetition 44

Reply All 51, 56

Reply in anger 51, 55

Report(s) .... vii, 39, 44, 48

Respond in kind 57

Rewriting viii

Rhetorical questions 48

Rhythm 78

Ronseal 76

Rules of grammar 11

S

Salutation 51, 53

Second draft 20

Self-critical 81, 83

Semco 34, 35

Semi-colons 47, 59, 60, 66

Semler, Ricardo 29, 34, 35, 56

Sentence(s) 11, 33

Short and to the point 10

Short paragraphs 29, 32, 45, 46, 47

Short sentences 29, 47

Short words 30, 31, 60

Showing your working 1, 20

Sidebars 49

Sign off 51

Simple constructions 18

Simple is best 69, 71

Simple language 14

Simple sentences 30

Simple words 18, 30

Singular verbs 37

Slide deck(s) 45, 48

Smiley faces 69

Social media 60

Speech marks 60

Speed of Eye-to-Brain Transmission
  (SEBT) 41

Spellcheck 49, 51, 54

Spelling 22, 60

Split infinitives 59, 63

Stark, Steven 14

Story's end 8

Strategy 13

Stream-of-consciousness 15

Style 22, 25, 31, 57, 77, 78

Sub-editor(s) 33, 42

Sub-head(s) 45, 46, 47

Subject 31

Subjective judgement 10

Sun, The 33, 36

Syntax 22

T

Taking criticism 7

Technical language 15

Text vii

Texting 60

The Seven Habits Of Highly Effective People 26

The way you write vii

Thesis 4

Think reader 7, 12

Time costs money 20

Tint 45, 49

Todd, Richard 19

Tone 51, 52, 53, 55, 57

Truss, Lynne 60

Twain, Mark 17, 27, 31

Tweet vii

Txt 57

Typefaces 35

Typesetters 21, 22

U

Ungrammatical 60

V

Verb(s) 11, 29, 31, 32, 33

Viral 52

Visual impact 46

Voice 78

W

What clients want 4, 10

What the reader wants ....
.... 7, 10, 12, 26, 31, 33, 52

What the customer wants 12

What we write doesn't please 7

White space 47

Who is your reader 1, 2

Why am I reading this? 7, 8

Why people read 1

Words 61

Writing at work 2, 3

Writing badly 18

Writing for clients 3

Writing for yourself 1, 3

Writing is never finished 12

Writing style 11

Writing to be assessed 3